The Gallows of New Brunswick
by Dorothy Dearborn
Illustrated by Carol Taylor

The Gallows of New Brunswick

A paperback original from Neptune Publishing Company Ltd.

10987654321
Copyright © 1999 by Dorothy Dearborn

The publisher wishes to acknowledge and thank the Department of Municipalities, Culture and Housing for their assistance in this publication.

Canadian Cataloguing in Publication Data

Dearborn, Dorothy
Gallows of New Brunswick
ISBN 1-896270-19-0

1. Hanging --New Brunswick. 2 Murder -- New Brunswick 1. Title

HV8579.D43 1999   364.66'092'27151   C99–950207–7

Cover Design by Dorothy Dearborn
Illustrations by Carol Taylor

Typesetting by Dearborn Group, Hampton, NB

Neptune Publishing Company Ltd.
Box 6941 Station A
Saint John, NB E2L 4S4

The Gallows of New Brunswick

Other books by Dorothy Dearborn

Non Fiction
New Brunswick Sea Stories
Neptune Publishing 1998
True Stories New Brunswickers at War
Neptune Publishing 1997
Legends Oddities Mysteries
... including UFO experiences in New Brunswick
Neptune Publishing 1996
New Brunswick's Unsung Heroes
Neptune Publishing 1996
Madness and Murder in New Brunswick
Neptune Publishing 1995
New Brunswick Ghosts Demons
and things that go bump in the night
Neptune Publishing 1994
Unsolved New Brunswick Murders
Neptune Publishing 1993

Biographies
Dyslexia Dr. Arthur Chesley, Saint John
Dearborn Group 1992
Give Me Fifteen Minutes Roy Alward of Havelock
Unipress Limited, Fredericton 1978

Collections
Partners in Progress, New Brunswick
Atlantic Canada–At the dawn of a New Nation
Windsor Publications Ltd. Burlington, Ontario, 1990

Anthologies
Willie, a short story
Stubborn Strength, A New Brunswick Anthology
Michael O. Nowlan, Academic Press Canada, 1983

Young Adult
The Secret of Pettingill Farms,
Avalon Books, New York 1972
The Mystery of Wood Island,
Avalon Books, New York 1973

Contents

Acknowledgements

The journalists of the 19th century were seldom named, their editors seldom acknowledged but the excellent work they did under what we would consider primitive circumstances today, made this book possible.

There were typewriters of sorts late in the century, there were telephones then, too. But throughout most of the period this book covers the telegraph was the main medium used to file a story in New Brunswick newspapers. Often important stories were received and printed on the day the action occurred, as extra editions if warranted. They could be stories from as far away as New York or Boston or as close to home as Campbellton, Fredericton, Moncton, Saint John or even smaller centres such as St. Stephen, Woodstock or Bathurst. Detailed and interesting accounts of events found their way across the telegraph wires to every corner of the province.

These events were not only reported but the local stories in particular were well written, specific and filled with information. Little was condensed, the writing was filled with colour and action, comments and presumptions. Reading this material was like being there, the depth far greater than today's television clip and most news stories.

Because of the dedication of those newspapers and their journalists we are able to understand how our ancestors felt 200 years ago when a murderer was loose in a community: To understand, not necessarily to agree with, the practice of hanging offenders ... both from the viewpoint of the community and of the culprit facing the gallows.

The events of this book are not the prettiest in our history but they do reflect an earlier, more simple time. Thanks to the newspapers of New Brunswick and their dedicated staff and thanks, too, to the always helpful staff of the Saint John Regional Library and the wonderful resources at our command.

Individuals, both friends and strangers, often come forward with information or items of interest that make a real contribution to my books. In this instance I am particularly indebted to Sgt. Pat Bonner of the Saint John City Police for sharing the drawing of the police station on King Street East: The same station where Canada's first city police force was founded in 1849.

A special thank you as well to my friend Paquerette Collins of Moncton and her friend Annette Hynes of Dalhousie for providing me with information on the hanging of Joseph Pierre Richard in Dalhousie, the last person to be hanged in New Brunswick.

POLICE STATION.

Saint John Police Station where Patrick Slavin was hanged from the window above the door at left in 1857. The station was home to Canada's first civic police force, formed in Saint John in 1849. The insert, above right, shows the area behind the gates where later hangings took place.
(Photo courtesy of Sgt. Pat Bonner, Saint John City Police Department.)

Preface

The idea for this book was due more to curiosity than any real interest in the business and, I discovered, the art, of hanging. Yes, that's right ... the art of hanging.

My original interest in the subject was piqued by recent mumblings about Canada returning to the death penalty for some crimes, primarily murders of the more heinous nature. Of course no one is pitching to bring back the noose, viewed as a rather barbaric form of execution. Modern "legal murders" tend to favour chemical injections ... like hanging, electrocution has been passé for decades.

Research into New Brunswick's history of hangings, and we have had our fair share over the last three centuries, has provided me with an opportunity to learn how both the public and the murderer viewed this form of punishment. I admit to being surprised to discover recalcitrant criminals walking to the gallows with their heads high and their hearts filled with the joy that comes from sparkling souls scrubbed clean, ready to meet their maker.

The business of hanging was a fairly lucrative one, the most successful hangmen succeeded in turning what was often perceived of as a ghoulish task into a work of art. The success of the hangman was based on his ability to effect a clean and quick kill. To this end more than one criminal has taken a very keen interest in who their hangman would be.

We've been led to believe that the rules called for the hangman to be anonymous to the victim, even at the very end and that most hangmen wore a black mask, not unlike the hood worn by the criminal at the time of his demise. It would seem that in Canada, at least in New Brunswick from what I can learn, this was not the case with the professionals. They took pride in their work and expected to be recognized for their skills. It was a great relief to Buck Whelan in the story, *I'm murdered, said Joe Steadman ... and he was* , to know who the hangman would be. Buck's friend Jim assured him that only the best had been brought in from Ontario to do the deed ... and Buck and the hangman actually bonded on the gallows.

Many hangmen took a scientific approach to the art of hanging an individual. It was a matter of mathematics as far as James Berry was concerned. He was so proud of his mastery of his trade that he left very detailed instructions in his memoirs for the use of his successors in the field. Using geometry, dynamics and mathematics Berry's rules were based on the "drop" method of hanging. The drop could be through the trap door of a gallows built for the occasion or from the second storey of a public building, such as the jailhouse in Saint John. The distance required in the drop was directly related to the weight of the person to be "dropped."

For example, according to Berry a "client" weighing 280 lbs will hit the bottom with almost double the force of one weighing 140 pounds but calculations must take into consideration the toughness or weakness of the "client's" neck.

Berry offered the following scale as a reasonably accurate guide: If a man weighed 196 pounds the amount of drop required would be eight feet to do the job properly; a 189 pound man would require eight feet, two inches and so on, down the scale with a 112 pound person requiring a 10 ft. drop.

The styles and methods of hanging varied from region to region as well. One method in New Brunswick was that used in St. Andrews where there actually was no drop but rather the victim was said to be "jerked to God." This particular method involved a series of pulleys and ropes arranged in such a way that, once the noose was properly secured, one strand of rope would be cut with a hatchet and the victim would be jerked heavenward as the noose tightened and his neck broke.

To allow a victim to strangle to death from hanging was considered a poor recommendation for a hangman.

One man's name became the symbol for the trade with the result that the hangman was frequently referred to simply as "Jack Ketch," a man said to be a master of the deadly trade.

The price of death by hanging was varied during the early years of our history. The theft of a shilling, interference with a landholding or intent to steal were as apt to result in a death penalty as would a murder.

For centuries the hanging itself was the centre of entertainment and enterprise in many communities. The public loved "a good hanging" and would begin arriving at the gallows long before dawn in order to get the best seats. In addition many entrepreneurs would take advantage of the crowds to hawk their wares.

The sheriff and his staff held the franchise for leasing out space around the scaffold to merchants who, in turn, erected their stands there and sold front row seats along with their merchandise. A brisk trade would be enjoyed and often a bit of entertainment by jugglers or magicians and the like ensued during the hours of waiting for the main attraction. The actual event, the hanging, lasted less than five minutes plus another 25 minutes until the body was examined and declared dead.

That thousands of people would be in attendance at a hanging in New Brunswick was not unusual. In 1857, when Patrick Slavin was hanged outside the jailhouse window on what is now King Street East in Saint John, it was estimated that close to 10,000 persons were on hand for the event. The area was so packed that the militia was called out to ensure orderly behaviour.

In fact people were encouraged to attend, the generally feeling was that watching a hanging reinforced both the penalty and the weight of the law.

In 1952, before hanging became passé in New Brunswick, the barristers here proposed that there should be one site selected for all New Brunswick hangings.

John T. Carvell told the Barristers' Society that "a great deal of horror" can be added to executions when county jail personnel are inexperienced in these grim duties.

"Mismanagement can be horrible and there has been mismanagement, I believe, on many occasions," he said.

Members of the society, with one exception, supported Carvell in his motion. The exception from the supporting vote said that in casting the negative vote he was opposing the punishment rather than the resolution itself.

When the vote was read by the president, R.D. Mitton of Moncton, S.G. Mooney of Andover wanted to know, "Does it mean all of us are in favour of hanging?"

"No!" the lawyers chorused in answer.

"I'm going to vote nay anyway," Mr. Mooney said.

The motion then went on to a discussion of whether the term "hanging" should be changed to "execution," brought forward by the then Attorney-General of the province, Hon. W.J. West, on the grounds that there might one day be a change in the form of the death sentence.

The report this comes from did not disclose whether the vote was carried or not, although the inference in the headline was that it was.

While we had our share of hangings in New Brunswick over the centuries we can't come near the record of Henry VIII during his reign, it is said there were 70,000 executions in that time. They were generally either hangings or beheadings.

Not to be outdone it should be noted that visitors to France in the 18th century were frequently appalled to discover half a dozen or more dead bodies broken on a wheel and a dozen or two bodies left hanging on triangular gallows along the roadside.

While records of multiple hangings in New Brunswick are rare it is interesting to note that as late as 1945 five men were hanged in Canada just before Christmas. One was a Canadian army veteran and the other four were German prisoners of war who had slain a fellow prisoner.

The headline in the *Chicago Times* of November, 1875 blazoned the words "Jerked to Jesus" noting that four Senegambian butchers "were wafted to heaven yesterday."

The record, however, probably goes to Fort Smith in 1875 when Judge Isaac C. Parker had a gallows erected long enough to accommodate 22 prisoners to be hanged at one time.

Rather a bloodthirsty bunch weren't we?

Woman indicted for murder
...New Brunswick's first serious crime

Nancy Mozely has the distinction of having committed the first major crime in the Province of New Brunswick and, while she was not found guilty of murder for impaling a pitch fork in her husband's head, her trial and subsequent punishment was too fascinating to ignore.

The warrant to apprehend Nancy reads:

To the Sheriff of the County of Sunbury, or his Deputy, or either of Constables of the Town of Parr, (later to become part of the City of Saint John)
Greeting:–
You are hereby commanded in His Majesty's name, to take the body of Nancy Mozely, a black woman, and bring her before me, or some other lawful authority, to answer to a complaint laid to her charge by Richard Cranker and Richard Wheeler for the murder of her husband, John Mozely, that she may be dealt with as the law directs. Fail not at your peril.
Given under my hand and seal this 6th day of October, 1784.
George Leonard,
Justice of the Peace.

Daniel Keefe, constable, served the warrant .

Richard Wheeler,John Walker and Jane Walker agreed to give evidence at the trial, having little choice with chattel mortgages placed on their property "for the use of His Majesty" should they fail to answer the court's questions or "depart without leave."

The medical examiner, Samuel Moore, carried out a post mortem and advised the court that he had "examined the black man's head. I am perfectly satisfied he was murdered. After examining where the fork perforated temporal bones of the skull, I sawed off the arch of the head and found the brain everywhere impacted with matter. The symptoms before death were also very obvious. All the jury were spectators."

The jury, "being duly qualified and duly sworn to examine the body of John Mozely, found dead, from the wounds of a fork in the head given him by his wife, accordingly we have examined the said body, and by the evidence sworn, find that the fork was the occasion of his death."

Amos Sheffield was the foreman and members of the jury were John Dan, William Sypher, William Crawford, Stephen Baxter, Henry Dickinson, William Scoby, John Kelsey, Hugh Brown, Isaac Inghram, John Miller and Peter Anderson.

As a result of these findings the first grand jury in the history of the province was summoned: Richard Lightfoot, John Hazen, John Boggs, John Kirk, John Smith, Oliver Arnold, Francis DeVeber, Caleb Howe, Daniel Melville, John Camp, Henry Thomas, John Ryan, William Harding, Thomas Mallard, Richard Bonsall, John Colville, James Ketcham, Luke D. Thornton, and Isaac Bell.

This jury found that Nancy Mozely "............ not having the fear of God before her eyes, but being moved and seduced by the instigation of the devil and of her malice aforethought, contriving and intending him, the said John Mozely, her said late husband, to deprive of his life and him traitorously to kill and murder on the twenty-seventh day of September, in the twenty-fourth year of the reign of our Sovereign Lord King George the Third .... then and there being feloniously, willfully and of her malice aforethought did make an assault, and that the said Nancy

Mozely, with a certain iron fork of the value of sixpence, which the said Nancy Mozely had held in her right hand, struck him, the said John Mozely, in and upon the head near unto the temple, and that the said John Mozely from the twenty-ninth day of October, in the same year at the Town of Parr aforesaid .... did languish, and of the mortal wound aforesaid on their oaths do say, that the said Nancy Mozely, the said John Mozely, her said husband, in manner and by means aforesaid, feloniously , traitorously, willfully and of her malice aforethought did kill and murder against the peace of our Lord and King, his Crown and dignity."

Then yet another jury, this the petit jury, was called and sworn to try the charge. Members of this jury included Frederick Devoe, Casper Doherty, Forbes Newton, James Picket, Jesse Marchant, John Wiggins, Abel Flewelling, Samuel Tilley, John Cooke, George Wilson, James Souvenir, Jeremiah Worden.

Nancy was brought before the petit jury and was found guilty of manslaughter. The next day she was brought to the bar yet again, this time she "prayed the benefit of clergy."

Benefit of clergy had its origin in the immunity ecclesiastics claimed and obtained in the days of ignorance and superstition. The clergy claimed exemption on Divine Authority, " touch not mine anointed" from being punished in civil courts.

Originally this privilege was only allowed to clerics but later every person who could read was considered to be a cleric, or clericus, and allowed the benefit of clergy even though they were not in holy orders.

The test of reading was applied when, upon conviction, a felon demanded his clergy, a book, often a psalter, was put into his hands and he was required to read it. One of the most common psalms was generally selected for the felon to read. The judge would then ask

15

the bishop's commissary who was present, "Legit ut Clericus?" His answer governed the prisoner's fate. If he found the prisoner "Non legit" then the punishment due him would be meted out.

The term "neck verse" is frequently used in relation to this reading, taken from King Lear: "Madame, I hope your Grace will stand between me and the neck verse if I am called in question for opening the King's letters."

When learning became more general, and the ability to read was no longer a proof of being in holy orders it was found that many laymen were admitted to the benefit of clergy. Eventually distinctions were made between scholars, real clerks or clergy; laymen were allowed benefit of clergy once and were then burnt with a hot iron in the brawn of the left thumb.

A statute passed during the reign of Queen Anne granted the benefit of clergy to all who were entitled to ask it, whether they could read or not. As a result persons convicted of manslaughter, grand larceny and other offenses were asked what they had to say, why judgment should not be pronounced against them. If in answer they "prayed the benefit of clergy" it would be granted them in such cases.

Nancy Mozely, therefore, was branded with an "M" on the meaty part of the thumb of her left hand and released from custody.

In later days in this new province others would pay for lesser crimes by hanging.

First trial and hanging ... at Fredericton

The first trial in Fredericton, that of David Nelson and William Harboard for the shooting of a native Indian in May of 1786, is of interest both for the fact of its call for the death penalty by hanging and because of the unusual politics which affected that decision.

We need to go back for about two years, to November of 1784, when a native, Charles Nichau Noiste, was tried and convicted in the Courts of Kings Bench at Quebec for the murder of Archibald McNeil at Madawaska.

(Quebec continued to claim jurisdiction in New Brunswick down to Grand Falls until 1792, when the governments of Quebec and New Brunswick were called on by the British government to adjust the lines between them.)

Noiste was found guilty and sentenced to be "hanged by the neck until he be dead."

Although he was subsequently executed for his crime Noiste was not hanged, as the sentence had demanded. Friends and relatives along with members of his, and of other aboriginal nations applied to Governor Frederick Haldimand to have the sentence commuted to death by shooting, a mode of execution "being more consonant to the idea of savages," according to reports at the time.

After consulting with Council at the Castle of St. Lewis, Quebec on November 3, 1784, as to "how far mercy ought to be extended in the way of changing the punishment, which was so earnestly prayed for," the Governor agreed to allow Noiste to be shot. "The Council having weighed the matter and the consequences that might ensue," were unanimous in their decision.

17

The Gallows of New Brunswick

The strength of the native bands at that time and the combined respect and fear in which they were held by the early settlers, were such that their demands were immediately granted. The execution of Noiste was accepted by the natives as fair punishment and was carried out according to their traditions.

This trial and execution had a strong influence on the final judgment in the sentencing of Nelson and Harboard, who were accused of having killed an Indian.

The two men, disbanded soldiers living on their farms in the Parish of Queensbury, 27 miles above Fredericton, were examined on May 24, 1786 by Hon. Isaac Allen and Hon. Edward Winslow, two of His Majesty's Justices of the Peace for the County of York. David Nelson testified that on the previous Saturday, "the sun being about half an hour high," he and Harboard went to the river to catch fish.

After being there a short time he said he heard dogs by the house after their hogs. Nelson said, "I dropped my pole and ran to the house for my forelock. When just above the house I found two dogs gnawing one of my hogs, which they had killed. When the dogs saw me they ran, and I fired at them. I spoke to William Harboard and desired him to fire, which he did, and killed one of the hogs.

"I then desired Harboard to go with me and see if other hogs were missing. We went, but could not find any. I then said the hogs must be taken into a boat. Whoever owns the boat must have the hogs. We then went to the shore and discovered some Indians about a quarter of a mile up the river. We beckoned to them to stop. They answered, 'No, no, and you have killed my dog.'

"I repeated to them to stop and said, 'You have killed my hogs'."

Then they pushed away across the river, which confirmed me in the opinion they had the hogs in the canoe.

"William Harboard then said, 'Let us fire over their heads, maybe they will hear the balls and come to'."

Upon which both men fired but Nelson claimed they had neither "design or intention of killing or wounding the persons in the canoe."

"I then loaded and fired the second shot for the same purpose. We then went again in search of our hogs and found all but one, which we supposed was in the canoe."

There were an Indian and his squaw in the canoe. One of the shots killed the Indian. His squaw then paddled the canoe to an island near an Indian encampment.

The following letter relative to the shooting was sent by Edward Winslow to Ward Chipman.

Fredericton, May 8, 1786

My Dear Chipman,

The enclosed letter to the Governor, with the examination contained therein, will explain to you a transaction which has been the source of great concern to our friend Col. Allen and myself. You will peruse the papers, seal the letter to the Governor and present it, and I expect of you that you will, on our behalf, urge the absolute necessity of the attendance of the Chief Justice.

The Indians on the one hand are clamorous for an instant decision. The multitude (I mean the people of the country) cannot reconcile themselves to the idea, that two men of fair character should be sacrificed to satisfy the barbarous claims of a set of savages. In this situation you will naturally suppose that we have had an arduous task to keep them quiet. We have assured both parties that the men will be fairly tried, and if guilty they will be punished. We have told them the Chief Justice must attend, and that he will set off as soon as he receives the information from us. I wish, when you deliver the Governor's letter, that you would suggest the peculiar situation of Col. Allen. the whole of the Indians are encamped around his house, and their rendezvous has already distressed his family and made them unhappy.

19

He had lately made a compact with them for a lot of land, and they think they have a right to call on him whenever they please. This event has increased their familiarity, and I believe if they had the idea he possessed the authority to decide in the present case, they would press him to peremptory decision, and if it was not agreeable to them, they might render the situation of the family very uncomfortable. I am not apt, you know, to anticipate evils, but I really believe the Indians would be troublesome on such an occasion. these considerations induce me to write thus ardently, that the Chief Justice will come, and that he come immediately. Impress this strongly on the Governor.

And now Chip, let me tell you one thing more. I think you should come to this country on some public occasion. Can a better offer than the present? The prosecutions are a matter of national expectation on one side, and of great concern on the other. Either the Attorney General or the Solicitor General must or ought to attend. Col. Allen authorizes me to tell you he has business of some consequence to engage you in. His gown and bands are at your house, his coat and waistcoat at Judge Putnam's. Pray don't forget them.

In haste, yours,

Edw. Winslow.

Ward Chipman, Esq.

The court opened at Fredericton June 14, 1786 with Chief Justice Ludlow and Judge Allen presiding. David Nelson and William Harboard were placed at the Bar for the shooting of the Indian. Ward Chipman produced his commission as Clerk of the Crown on the Circuits, and conducted the prosecution.

The prisoners were not defended by counsel, it not being allowed to persons charged with capital offenses.

The petit jury, the first at Fredericton, was made up of the following persons: Cornelius Thompson, George Cox,

George B.Rodney, Jacob Blacker, Xenophen Jewett,William Gevard, Joseph Harrison, Isaac Benson, Charles Mathewson, John Jewett, Josiah Barker and Francis Stephenson.

Three witnesses were called, one being Edward Winslow, who had assisted in taking the preliminary examination of the prisoners, to prove their statements before the justices of the peace, and that they were made voluntarily, in which case they would be evidence against the prisoners.

They were both found guilty of shooting the Indian, and sentenced to be hanged June 23, nine days after the opening of the court, and less than one month after the shooting of the Indian. Jonathan Sewell wrote the following letter relative to them:

Fredericton, 6 July, 1786

Dear Sir–

Poor Harboard has been out of his senses. When told he was reprieved, he replied that he had suffered what was worse than death, and was perfectly indifferent about his execution. He is now at liberty , and at his former home. Parson Beardsley did not think proper to attend the unfortunate Nelson the day of his execution, although he was, as you remember, particularly requested.

Yours truly,
Jonathan Sewell Jr.

The belief was general that if Nelson had not been executed the Indians would have had revenge but, seeing justice done, they were ever peaceable.

Unlucky horse shoes

There were times, during the early years of Loyalist settlement in New Brunswick, when trial and judgement were swift: Particularly when it involved slaves.

In this instance a slave of Judge Upham, a Massachusetts Loyalist who made his home at Hammond River, near Hampton, was tried for the murder of "the girl West."

At the St. John Circuit Court in September of 1798, with Judge Allen on the Bench, Luke Hamilton was tried for murder. He was reputed to be returning to "the residence of his master, Hammond River, when he met the girl picking berries, two miles from the city near the Old Westmorland Road."

Luke did not, of course, enter a plea, he would have had little say in the matter of his guilt or innocence in those days. He was convicted from the marks of the horse shoes on the ground near where the body of the girl was found.

Luke was executed. We presume the execution was the popular one of hanging.

Religious Fervour in Shediac

In the spring of 1804 a revival took place among the Baptist people in the settlement of Shediac. At first, meetings were held on Sunday evenings but as the interest in the community grew they were held on Thursday nights as well. By autumn the enthusiasm among the revivalists was even more intense and the people reached a high pitch of excitement, many of them were convinced the world was coming to an end. Interpretations attached to prophetic portions of both the Old and New Testaments ran rampant.

Travelling Baptist preachers added their fervour to the constantly growing excitement. Two young men on their way to Prince Edward Island held a revival meeting that lasted all night ...... and still the fervour grew until, history tells us, the community was more than ready for one Jacob Peck who came through from Shepody in January of 1805. The extravagance of Peck's appeals to the excitable nature of his hearers is said to have exceeded any of his predecessors.

His "lurid declamation seems to have been all that was needed to drive a number of people out of their minds," as he proceeded to preach hellfire and damnation day and night to all who would listen to him ... and many did.

Among them were Amasa Babcock, his daughter Sarah, and Sarah Cornwall. The Babcock girl fell into a trance and began to prophesy that the end of the world was at hand and those present, particularly Jacob Peck, wanted the prophesy committed to paper but no one present at the assembly was able to take it down.

The girls were presumed to be dying and an excited gathering summoned Mr. William Hannington to take their deposition. At first he refused to go, sending the message that

23

it was "all a delusion," and telling his wife that "they wanted mad houses, not meeting houses."

Hannington held Church of England services in his home on Sundays, and was not sympathetic to the methods adopted in the revivalist services. The people, however, believed that these unbalanced minds were inspired and were anxious to have the prophecies preserved. They persisted in requesting Mr. Hannington's presence, saying that the girls had something to say "before they died" and they wanted it written down.

Mr. Hannington, who had gone to bed by this time, consented to go, telling his wife that perhaps he could "convince them of their error."

He found the girls lying on a bed and Jacob Peck pacing to and fro in the room repeating, "there is my epistle," and pointing to the two girls.

In resignation Mr. Hannington inquired what the girls had to say and proceeded to commit the so-called prophesy to writing, the gist of which was that Mr. Hannington was to be converted, and Jacob Peck and the prophetesses were to convert the French.

Amasa Babcock was a man of middle life with a wife and nine children, the family lived on the road to Cocagne. His oldest child was twenty and the youngest was an infant. His sister, Mercy Hall, who had been married to a man not then living with her, was one of the family. She was described as being of a " melancholy disposition" and was not allowed to eat with the family.

Mr. Hannington liked Babcock and had bought a place for him with the understanding that he was to be paid in gaspereaux, which Babcock was to catch. Babcock had not been terribly successful in catching the gaspereaux so Hannington had given him some young cattle to winter for him but a neighbour, Joseph Poirier, told Hannington that his cattle were suffering for want of food.

That day, February 13, 1892 Hannington told Babcock

After taking off his shoes and going out in the snow Amasa came back in the house and arranged his family on a long bench against the wall ... he took up a clasp knife and began to whet it on a whetstone, he then went to his sister Mercy and told her to prepare for death.

what Poirier had said. Babcock replied, "the Lord will provide."

Hannington told Babcock if he did not go home he would take the cattle from him.

Babcock went home that night and took his brother Jonathan with him to grind grain in a hand mill.

As Jonathan ground the grain Amasa took the flour and sprinkled it on the floor saying, "this is the bread of heaven."

According to his wife's statement Amasa then took off his shoes and went out into the snow crying out, "the world is coming to an end, and the stars are falling."

He then came back to the house and arranged his family on a long bench against the wall, the eldest girl at one end, and his wife and youngest child at the other. He took up a clasp knife and began to whet it on a whetstone. Going over to his sister Mercy he commanded her to remove her dress, get on her knees and prepare for death, for her hour was come. He next ordered his brother Jonathan to strip himself and, so infatuated were they that both meekly obeyed.

Amasa began acting like someone possessed of the devil. He went to the window and looked out several times, as if expecting something to happen. Then he laid his knife down on the floor on top of a whetstone calling out, "The cross of Christ" while stamping on the whetstone until he broke it after which he picked up the knife and went over to where his naked sister was kneeling and stabbed her with the knife. She fell to the floor, the blood gushing from the wound, and died in a few minutes.

This brought the family to their senses. As soon as Jonathan saw the blood flow he opened the door and fled, naked, to the house of Joseph Poirier, a quarter of a mile away. There he was supplied with clothes before going along to Mr. Hannington's house. He aroused Hannington by crying out that his brother, Amasa, had stuck his sister with a knife.

There was no magistrate at Shediac and at first Hannington refused to arrest Amasa Babcock but he finally agreed to go to his house.

There were no public roads to travel so, at about two o'clock in the morning, Hannington put on snowshoes and started out first for Joseph Poirier's house. When he arrived he asked Poirier where his brothers Pascal and Chrysostom were. He was told they were at their father's home so Hannington went there and asked the two young men to accompany him to Amasa Babcock's house.

When they arrived they found Amasa walking about with his hands clasped.

Hannington told the Poirier boys to seize him.

Babcock resisted and wanted to know what they were going to do with him. He was told he was to be held a prisoner.

Babcock then cried out, "Gideon's men arise!" At which his two younger sons, Caleb and Henry jumped to their feet but were quickly made to sit down again.

Mrs. Babcock was asked if her sister-in-law was dead and she said, "Yes."

Around sunrise some of the English-speaking people in the community arrived and Mercy's body was found in the snowdrift where Amasa had taken it.

Amasa's hands were then strapped and he was taken to Mr. Hannington's. When he arrived he cried out, "Aha! Aha! It was permitted."

The necessary papers were got out on the information provided by Jonathan Babcock as eyewitness to the crime.

Amasa cried out again, "These are letters from Damascus, send them to Damascus," apparently alluding to Saul's persecution of the Christians.

He was taken to the home of Amasa Killam where, because he became quite crazed from time to time, he was placed on a bed, his arms pinioned and fastened down on the floor.

On the third day, when the weather improved, they put straps around his arms again, placed him on a light sled and snowshoed to Dorchester, hauling the sled by hand.

Amasa Babcock was then indicted for the murder of his sister, Mercy. Upon a true bill being found he was tried at court in Dorchester on June 15, 1805 before Judge Upham and a large turnout of spectators.

The prosecuting officer was Ward Chipman, clerk of the Crown on the Circuit. The trial lasted six hours. It took the jury only half-an-hour to return a verdict of guilty. Amasa

Babcock was sentenced to be executed on Friday, June 28.

No one in attendance voiced any opposition to the sentence.

In the book, *Judges of New Brunswick* one of the contributors notes that "the motive of the perpetrator of this terrible crime, although vague, was not vulgar or sordid, and was apparently based upon a fanatical misconception of religious duty.

"Contrasting this case with cases of the same nature occurring in modern times (The book *The Judges of New Brunswick* was published in 1907) the most striking feature connected with the former is the apparent absence of any attempt to contend that Babcock was not responsible for his hideous act.

"Although much may be said against the undue use of refined arguments tending to relieve accused persons of a criminal intent, when it obviously exists, or of criminal responsibility for which should not be denied, there can scarcely be a question that no tribunal of today would hold one in Babcock's position guilty of murder, or would be justified of so doing."

On Wednesday, June 26, 1805, the Daily Transcript carried the following report of the Babcock event:

On Saturday the 15th inst. at a Court of Oyer, and Terminer and Goal delivery, holden at Dorchester, for the County of Westmorland, at which his Honour Judge Upham presided, came on the trial of Amasa Babcock for the murder of his sister Mercy Hall, at Chediac (sic) in that County, on the 13th day of February last; the trial lasted about six hours when the jury, after retiring half-an-hour, returned with a verdict of guilty against the prisoner, he was thereupon sentenced for execution on Friday the 28th instant.

It appeared in evidence that for some time before the murder was committed, the prisoner with several of his neighbours, had been in the habit of meeting under a pretence of religious exercises at each other's houses, at which one Jacob Peck was a principal performer; that they were under strong delusion and conducted themselves in a very frantic, irregular and even impious manner, and that in consequence of some pretended prophesies by some of the company in their pretended religious phrenzies against the unfortunate deceased; the prisoner was probably induced to commit the horrid, barbarous and cruel murder of which he was convicted.

The concourse of people at the trial was very great, who all appear to be satisfied of the justice of the verdict and sentence.

The above-named Jacob Peck was on the same day indicted for blasphemous, profane and seditious language at the meetings above-mentioned, and recognised with good sureties to appear at the next Court of Oyer and Terminer in that County, to prosecute his traverse to the said indictment with effect.

It is hoped and expected that these legal proceedings will have a good effect in putting an end to the strange and lamentable delusion, which made them necessary, and brought the unhappy culprit to such an ignominious death.

Babcock was duly hanged on the designated date of June 28, 1805. Since no family member claimed the remains his body was unceremoniously wrapped and buried in Dorchester, beneath the gallows which claimed that miserable life and deranged mind.

A loaf of bread + 25 cents = one noose on Feb.21, 1824

The Citizen, published in the mid-1980s by Saint John entrepreneur and developer Pat Rocca, was a short-lived but lively weekly newspaper filled with local columns and comments. Among these was a regular column contributed by local historian Frank O'Brien. The following appeared May 13, 1986 and was titled:

Boy Hanged for Stealing a Loaf of Bread

According to O'Brien, "details of this disgraceful miscarriage fill the blackest page in Saint John history, and to think it had to happen on our most honoured spot, where the Loyalists stepped ashore.

"Those most guilty of the outrage offer these rather silly qualifications: The victim, aged 18, was no mere boy, and he broke into two houses and stole additional articles. They ought to have known that sentences are measured simply in relation to the offence for which the person has been convicted, in this case 25 cents."

The loaf of bread was a previous offence.

In his work, *Footprints*, historian J.W. Lawrence gave the following brief account of what, incidentally, was the last trial for a capital offence to be held in Saint John's old Court House.

During the January 1828 term, with the Hon. Judge Ward Chipman presiding, "Patrick Burgen, aged 18 years, of York Point was placed at the Bar, charged with entering the dwelling, in the night, of his master, John B. Smith, manufacturer of ginger beer, corner of Union Street and Drury Lane, and robbing the till of one quarter of a dollar. He was arrested the day after by John McArthur, constable."

The prosecuting officer was Clerk of the Crown John Thomas Murray, Esq. The Court assigned William B. Kinnear as counsel for the prisoner.

Lawrence makes this brief reference to the legal process of the time: "... as to questions of law, not being allowed then to refer to questions of fact or address the Jury."

Members of the jury included John Cunningham, foreman; Gilbert T. Ray, Isaac Flewelling, William Cormick, M.J. Lowrey, Nehemiah Vail, Amos Robertson, Wm. Stout, George Hutchinson, David Schurman, James Rankin, William B. Cox.

"As the evidence of guilt was clear no other course was open to the Jury than a verdict of 'Guilty,' with this was a recommendation to mercy. Yet, the Judge, in sentencing the prisoner to be executed, told him there was no hope for mercy and he should lose no time in preparing for death."

A petition was sent to the Lieutenant-Governor, Sir Howard Douglas, asking the interposition of the prerogative in behalf of the prisoner. Yet, notwithstanding the recommendation of the jury and the coronation oath of the sovereign, requiring: "His Majesty to cause Law and Justice in Mercy to be executed in all his judgements. The law was allowed to take its course, and Patrick Burgen was executed on the 21st day of February, 1828, from the second storey window of the "Old Gaol."

The executioner was Blizard Baine, an Englishman undergoing a sentence of two years for robbery. In addition to release from prison he received 10 pounds from Sheriff White. Baine lost no time in leaving the city. White, realizing the hangman's life was now not worth a loaf of bread, let him out of the back door of the jail late that night with the warning, "Get out of town as fast as you can, sneak through the back streets because if they catch you they will literally tear you to pieces."

The Gallows of New Brunswick

OLD CITY HALL.

*For nearly one third of a century
(from 1797 until 1830) the above building
on Saint John's Market Square was called
the City Hall. The basement at first was a general
store; the first flat, with entrance from King Street
was occupied as the City Market; the upper storey
with a platform the length of the building was used for
the Courts and Council Chamber.
There has been reference to the fact that
hangings were frequently carried out using the above
building as a convenient "drop off" for the hangman's
noose. Patrick Burgen, of loaf-of-bread fame, was said to
have been executed on the 21st day of February, 1828,
by being hanged from the second storey window.*

(The above illustration is from Lawrence's book Footprints.)

O'Brien claimed Sheriff White would never have anything to do with Chipman after that. He went on to say, "Admittedly, sentences for burglary had to be severe due to the fact that householders were very vulnerable. People were not yet accustomed to using the one bank in town at that time and kept their entire life savings at home. Their amount of security may be judged by the fact that a single watchman patrolled the whole of Carleton. Therefore justice had to be rigorous, but definitely not so harsh as that inflicted on poor Burgen."

Stephen Humbert, an early Methodist in the city of Saint John, who was elected to the House of Assembly of New Brunswick several times during the first quarter of the Nineteenth Century, also appears to have been associated with this story. David G. Keirstead of Hampton found the following quotation while doing genealogical research on Humbert, his great, great, great- grandfather, and presented it to the Kings County Historical Society along with O'Brien's story.

Humbert "was known as a man who stood firmly for everything in which he believed and who was not afraid to voice his opinion. There has always been a tradition in his family that he protested vigorously against the hanging of a man (some say two men) convicted of stealing a loaf of bread, and that he walked to the scaffold with the unfortunate young man to show his sympathy with him and his disapproval of the severe sentence."

Another book at the New Brunswick Museum, tells of another time when Stephen Humbert was involved with hangings in Saint John, according to Keirstead.

"His religion was active – not passive. When the condemned murderers of an innkeeper in Musquash were marching to the gallows on King Street East in 1808, Stephen Humbert walked with them, singing Methodist hymns.

"Executions were not private in those days. The

hanging of criminals sentenced by the court was considered a salutary lesson to the public.

"There never was any lack of a crowd. On this particular occasion there was plenty to talk about afterwards for the ropes used for the execution broke on the first attempt to hang the murderers, who were then compelled to wait until stronger ones were obtained from the South Wharf where the ship chandlery stores were located.......

"It is said that the bodies of both men so executed were buried at the foot of the gallows, which was erected at what is now the foot of King Street East, between Pitt and Crown Streets." (From a presentation by David Keirstead, Hampton, May 17, 1986)

The Gallows of New Brunswick
Cold blooded horror shocks Saint John in 1857

6,000 spectators watch Patrick Slavin hanged from window of Saint John jail

Cold blooded horror
shocks Saint John

This story has been written about over and over again as journalists and historians find themselves intrigued with its almost unbelievable cold blooded, horror. Were it not for evidence at the trial that leaves little doubt as to what happened on that fateful Saturday night the most creative imaginations could not, would not, write of such a scene of carnage.

The murder of Robert McKenzie and his family is the stuff that folk tales are made of. We offer a brief account here, as gleaned from New Brunswick newspapers at the time. **dd**

In 1857 Robert McKenzie was known as a wealthy man. He had operated a successful tailoring business in Saint John for a number of years before deciding to retire to a farming life in Mispec, a sparsely populated community 10 miles or so outside the city. His nearest neighbour was Peter Hare who lived about a mile down the road.

McKenzie lived with his family, a wife and four children, in the main farm house and he owned a second, smaller house across the road which he made available to his "hired hand."

In the fall of 1857 a man calling himself by the name "Williams" talked to McKenzie about becoming that hired hand and did, eventually, come to an agreement with him. He was expected to move into the small house by November 1.

Williams' real name was Hugh Breen and he had no intention of doing an honest day's work on McKenzie's farm. His sole purpose in calling on McKenzie was to "suss out" the lay of the land for he and one Patrick Slavin who believed McKenzie's wealth, in the form of gold coins, was contained in a strong box or safe somewhere on the premises.

On the Saturday night Breen, Slavin and Slavin's son Patrick Junior headed for the McKenzie property. Breen's role was to lure McKenzie out to the smaller house, on the pretext of some questions to be asked prior to moving his family there that weekend.

Once they lured McKenzie outside the mayhem and destruction began. The following verbatim description, given in court by an eyewitness who visited the scene to help identify the dead is horrid enough, Slavin's own description of the killing spree will shake the most blasé reader.

During Slavin's and Breen's trial William Reed, brother of McKenzie's wife, was questioned by the solicitor general. This is his statement:

"I helped to search the ruins. Both houses were consumed (by fire). In the little house was found a body, with some flesh, though the head and legs were gone. The trunk, without arms, remained. There was some flesh on it. We could tell it was a male but there was nothing to identify it with McKenzie. It was lying in the southwest corner of the smaller house. Lime and ruins of the building were on it. We discovered nothing more to that house.

"In the other house we discovered bones. They were completely burned up. We found a woman's head and a heart but nothing by which we could identify the remains. The limbs and head were all gone. The child's head, legs and arms were gone. It was very small. The eldest child was five years old on the 3rd last September. The other three were younger. I could not form an idea of the age of the youngest child. I found the remains in the iron chest. The key was in the chest but the door was open. It was about two o'clock when I arrived there."

In his testimony during the trial Old Slavin matter-of-factly bragged of his accomplishments on that day.

"It was myself was the head, and foundation and back-setting of robbing and murdering McKenzie," he said.

Originally they had planned the murdering of the McKenzie family for earlier in the week but the hired hand, named Polley, was still working there and Slavin didn't want to kill Polley. They then decided on Thursday but, Slavin said, Breen had learned that George Leet and his wife were coming that evening and that delayed things once more.

Finally, on the Saturday, they set off, Slavin, Breen and Slavin's eldest son Pat. Slavin bragged that he didn't ask either of the others for help "knowing I was able to put it through myself."

They went to the "lower" house where Breen set a fire in the fireplace then went to get McKenzie.

"I had no intention but to take his life."

Slavin hid in the bedroom and when McKenzie and Breen came into the kitchen "I walked out of the bedroom and I said nothing, but struck him on the breast with the poll of the axe. He fell. That blow did not kill him exactly. I struck him five or six times on the head and breast and wherever it was at hand."

He then searched the body for the more than £100 McKenzie was rumoured to always carry on him. They didn't find a farthing.

After throwing McKenzie's body in the cellar Slavin and Breen then went up to the main house "to kill what was in it and rob the house."

Breen stopped to have a few words with Mrs. McKenzie who was expecting him that evening to talk about the farm-hand job, he then stepped aside and handed Slavin an axe that was standing beside the door.

"There was a bright light," Slavin said. "I saw Mrs. McKenzie sitting on a rocking chair with a child in her arms, there were four children altogether. When I went in I did not speak but just struck her on the side of the head, by the ear, with the axe. She struggled a good deal. She died very hard.

"I think the child was killed in striking at the mother. The children screamed and cried a little. They did not run away but kept about the mother. I killed them with my own hand. I killed the whole lot of them."

After the killing spree the men searched the house, disappointed not to find the fortune McKenzie was said to keep at home. Old Slavin did find £100 in gold, kept in a cotton purse.

After gathering up whatever items they wanted and moving McKenzie's body up from the cellar the men then set about setting fire to both houses before heading back to the Slavin house.

Old Slavin was not impressed with either of his helpers, "They weren't fit to do anything. ....I have it all on me."

He went on to say that, although they had gone into the woods around the Slavin home, they had no intention of attempting to run away.

"I'm just as well satisfied I didn't escape. I killed all the concerned and I think I ought to die for it. ... I am satisfied to swing for it."

The major witness at their trial was one of Slavin's younger sons who described the scene when Slavin, Breen and young Pat arrived home late Saturday night. His testimony, although he was only ten years-old was so credible the judge readily accepted it as true.

John Slavin told the court, "I am ten years old. Can tell the truth and the whole truth. Have heard of Heaven and of Hell. Know it is wrong not to tell the truth. My father's name is John (Patrick) Slavin. That is Pat, my brother. I live on Loch Lomond Road. Father, mother, Pat ...... live there. I do not know my sister's name. Never saw her. She is in the old country. Have a younger brother named Jimmy. There is no sister living at home. Never knew Breen 'til I see'd him five weeks ago. Saw him at father's house. Heard of McKenzie's house being burned. He was in the house four weeks before that. He was living and sleeping there. Pat was living there during that time. McKenzie's house was burned on Saturday. Saw Breen in the morning. Saw father and Patrick that day. Father, Pat and Breen were not at home when I went to bed on Saturday. I saw them at one o'clock. I was at home from that time till I went to bed. I saw them leave the place together. They said they were going to Black River. They said nothing else.

"Next saw them the same night. They came back about a couple of hours after dark. I was in bed. The three of them came in. I was awake. They had a white bag with them. A middling small one. There were clothes in it. Socks and a pair of boots were in it. My father said they got the things at McKenzie's. He was speaking to the whole of them. My mother was present. They took their suppers then. After supper they counted the money. It was gold. Father took it out. He said there were 50 sovereigns. Father gave all I saw to my mother. When they came in she was not very well pleased with them. She called them rascals. They said she would not get any money. That was before I saw the money.

"Saw a watch. Father had it. It was yellow. Saw a purse with them. They said they set McKenzie's house on fire. My father said that Breen said nothing. Patrick said nothing. My father said they killed McKenzie. My father said he hit him with the axe. He said he killed the woman then. He said he killed the children then. Did not hear Breen or Pat say anything when father said this."

Young John watched the men all the next day as they took their loot into the woods to hide it and he watched from a vantage point as his brother Pat who had, he said, "10 pieces. I saw them. He had more in the pocket book. It was a square black one."

Mr. Kerr, Slavin's lawyer, appealed for young Slavin's life, suggesting he was too simple-minded to have formed a clear idea of what the men were about to do. He compared the youth's upbringing to that of a dog reared by a cruel and exacting master.

Charles Fisher, acting for the Crown, said the evidence impressed on him the conviction that the boy was of a most diabolical nature and was "not fit to be set loose in this country."

Judge Parker noted that Patrick was charged with aiding and abetting the actual murders and that anyone within sight and hearing of such, or who keeps watch, is guilty in the second degree and liable to the penalty attending murder. The question the jury must ask, he said, is whether or not young Slavin had the mental capacity to distinguish right from wrong, whether he was so wanting in sense that he could not be held criminally responsible for his acts.

Young John Slavin's evidence was lengthy and damning and, when the trial was over, the jury found the two men guilty of murder, but retired again to give their decision on the fate of young Patrick.

"Patrick Slavin (Senior) and Hugh Breen," the clerk addressed them, "what have you to say why sentence of death should not be passed on you?"

"I'm satisfied sir," said old Slavin.

Breen said nothing.

"The extent of your crime," the judge said, "is fearful to contemplate. It is such as was never before known in this, and perhaps not in any other country."

Judge Parker then held them as "a terror and warning to all evil-minded persons." And sentenced both to hang on Friday, December 11, 1857.

The jury returned after considering young Patrick's case and announced a verdict of "guilty." He was then remanded until Friday November 20 when he appeared for sentencing. Throughout the trial and the sentencing he showed no indication of any understanding of what was going on around him or concerning him.

"Patrick Slavin Junior," the judge said, "you stand in as dreadful a position as any man can stand." He then proceeded to outline and itemize both the crime and young Patrick's part in it and in all the horror. Eventually he got to the matter of leniency recommended by the jury, noting that it was based on the boy's age, ignorance and the dreadful example set by his father.

"I have not thought it inconsistent with my duty to recommend to His Excellency, the Lieutenant-Governor ... that mercy be extended to you. I can now give you hope that your life will be spared."

Whereupon he urged Patrick to put his life to whatever good use he might in a lifetime behind bars, whereupon he sentenced him to life in prison.

Part Two
The Hanging

On Saturday, December 18, 1857 the *Carleton Senti-nel*, published in Woodstock, NB noted the excitement that had prevailed in Saint John during the previous week, aris-ing from the imprisonment of Breen and Slavin and, in par-ticular the death of Breen.

From the beginning Slavin had disparaged Hugh Breen for the coward he was, and continued to be, throughout the trial and, particularly, after being sentenced to hang on De-cember 11. Because of Breen's reputation his jailers saw no need to place a guard inside the cell with the man, a guard outside was deemed to be sufficient for someone who continued to bewail his fate and gradually fell into deep depression. Obviously such a person lacked the bravery required to either escape or commit suicide.

A Mrs. Doherty, one of Breen's visitors, was serving as his guard on Sunday December 6 while the daughter of Nugent Creighton, the jailer, who generally occupied this post, went for her supper. At about 6:30 p.m. Mrs. Doherty left without notifying anyone. When the Creighton girl re-turned she spoke to Breen through the wicket of the cell door but got no reply. She peered through the wicket and could see him lying partially on his cot at the furthest length of the chain that bound one of his legs to a bolt in the cen-tre of the floor, his head was in a corner beyond the end of the cot.

The girl made a hasty entry and discovered that Breen, obviously in terror of the hangman, had turned hangman himself.

To accomplish the act Breen had managed to get a piece of wood about a yard long and placed it in the corner so that one end was supported on a cleat in the wall while the other rested on a nail in the adjacent wall. He then made a noose from a handkerchief which he tied to his gallows-tree following which he thrust his head through the loop and allowed himself to fall forward until, under the weight of his own body, he choked to death.

While the coroner's jury censured the sheriff and jail officials for negligence ... in allowing Breen the chance to escape a paid hangman ... no other action was taken.

The *Carleton Sentinel*, however, saw religious bigotry playing a role in this suicide by noting that "Protestants were as much as possible excluded and one gentleman, who had been sent for by Breen and who, on conversing with him through the wicket endeavoured, as any Christian would, to give the culprit advice suited to his position was assailed by the young woman in attendance in coarse and unfeeling language, and told that none of his preaching was wanted there – that Breen had his own spiritual advisor."

The paper goes on to note that a lady – "one of his spiritual advisers – had been with him in his cell from half-past two o'clock until half-past six o'clock on Sunday afternoon. Twenty minutes after the lady left the gaoler's daughter discovered Breen dead.

"Whether the action resulted from a far-fetched religious plot or from Breen's cowardly behaviour is lost in history today, and good riddance, too. Breen simply managed to do the hangman out of his fee."

Not so Patrick Slavin Senior.

On December 10 the carpenters set about the job of building a gallows on the jail at Great George Street, now known as King Street East, in Saint John. It was described as a gibbet made of four strong beams set on end with side ties and a centre crosspiece on the top of a height that would bring the platform on a level with the sill of the large window over the jail door. The drop consisted of a simple flap board, hinged at one side like the half of an ordinary hatch, supported at the other end by two stout ropes passing over the top piece of the structure and attached to a cleat inside. By this means all that was necessary was to cut the rope close to the fastening with the stroke of a hatchet. When the drop fell it left the standing place of the culprit an empty void. A simple and efficient arrangement.

Crowds began to gather at an early hour in front of the jail for this public hanging. With the exception of the man with the hatchet, who would cut the rope, everyone was in public view.

The day dawned clear and cold and there was a little snow on the ground. The hanging was set for ten o'clock in the morning but people, memories still vivid with the horror of Patrick Slavin's crime, were there by dawn.

There was Mayor George Blatch, the local magistrates and dignitaries galore among the estimated five or six thousand who filled even the adjacent streets, the Old Burying Ground and King's Square. They were anywhere and everywhere that offered a view of the high gallows. To ensure proper order every available policeman and military individual was ringed about the gallows, members of the 62nd Regiment were armed with guns with bayonets fixed.

At ten minutes past ten o'clock old Slavin appeared in the company of High Sheriff Charles Johnson and Rev. John Sweeney, a Roman Catholic priest. Slavin walked steadily, spoke to no one, and stood quietly on the trap. Police Constable Pigeon came forward and slipped the black hood on Patrick Slavin's head and the sheriff then fitted the noose in place.

As the priest began a prayer the sheriff stepped back into the jail and, a moment later, the trap fell.

It was called "a good job." Slavin's neck was dislocated in the fall and the only motion beneath the drop was a momentary jerking of one leg. The body hung for 35 minutes before being examined by Doctors Hairs and Travers and cut down .

The people slowly and quietly moved away from the awesome spectacle.

Love triangle?

Thomas Dowd was a small man of rather slight build with straight black hair, wrinkled forehead, deep-set dull eyes, a heavy mouth and a thick, short moustache and goatee mixed with grey. He was known in the community as a "casual worker" who boarded at the Ward house.

The above description was carried in the *St. John Globe* during the inquest into the violent death of Thomas Edward Ward of New River, Charlotte County on September 9, 1878.

Dowd and a young man in his twenties, David McCarthy, were boarders at the Ward home which included Thomas, Elizabeth and their daughters, 17 year-old Annie and four year-old Susan.

It was a small home wrought with big problems, among them suspicion of at least one love triangle, involving Mr. and Mrs. Ward and Tom Dowd, and a sexual relationship between Annie Ward and David McCarthy. Alcohol fuelled the flames of love and hate on a regular basis, eventually leading Thomas Ward to attempt to set his house in order. Not an easy chore for the 63 year-old man who had complained to neighbours on more than one occasion of his much younger wife's behaviour with Dowd.

Ward left his home in the early morning of Sept. 9, intent on doing some bridge repairs across a stream half a mile away, before pitching some hay in a nearby pasture. He carried with him an axe and a pitchfork.

Thomas Dowd left the house twenty minutes earlier than Ward, his intent was to go berry-picking in some bushes lining a pasture south of the house.

Ward did not return home that day, nor the next, and Elizabeth offered a number of explanations for his absence.

Claiming at one time that he had taken his good clothes on Sunday night and left her and, at another time, simply saying he had gone to cut hay and had not come back.

The previous evening Ward had been drinking and had banished his daughter Annie from the house on the grounds that she was sleeping with McCarthy. When Elizabeth went to the neighbours where Annie was staying she was rumoured to have said her husband had "gone to where he wouldn't trouble her (the daughter) any more." She made no efforts to find her husband.

Nearly a week later Thomas Mulherrin and other of the residents of New River went to Lepreaux (sic) and laid the matter of Ward's disappearance before Squire Reynolds who suggested a search of the neighbourhood should be made.

Four men, Mulherrin, Richard Lynch, Fred McMaster and one other started out on a searching expedition. They took the meadow path and spread themselves about the immediate locality. It wasn't long before McMaster discovered an unbearable smell coming from a clump of bushes. One of the group approached closer and discovered the body of the murdered man.

Thomas Ward was stretched on his back and covered with underbrush and moss, his feet were protruding.

The men were so horror-stricken that they refused to touch the remains and hastened to Lepreaux to inform Reynolds of the success of their search.

Reynolds, who was also the local coroner, drove up to New River and directed two constables to guard the body and two others to watch Mrs. Ward and "secure the person of Thomas Dowd."

Dowd, however, had left the Ward home on Thursday and gone to Musquash and was found in the home of a man named Foley. He was about to go to bed when the constables arrived and informed him that he was a prisoner. He asked no questions but dressed quickly and placed himself in the charge of the officers.

On the road to Lepreaux he was cool and collected and denied all knowledge of the crime.

The body was allowed to remain in the bushes where it was discovered until Coroner Reynolds' jury, composed of Oscar Hanson, foreman, C.F. Clinch, Robert Dixon, Patrick Daly, William Chittick, James Boyne and G. Gammel, had time to view it.

When the brush and moss was removed a "horrible sight" was presented to them. The murdered man lay flat on his back, with one arm drawn over his head. His shirts were drawn up showing that he had been dragged by the feet from the place where he had been killed.

An examination of the head showed a fracture of the skull, evidently the effect of a very heavy blow. The bone was smashed in and cracked. The corpse was altogether unrecognizable. The flesh had been eaten off the face and off the body by myriads of beetles, the ribs were quite bare and the teeth protruded – making the spectacle one of the most ghastly imaginable.

Relatives of Ward were brought to the area to identify the body. Annie Ward was quite broken up and refused for a long to time to even look at the remains. Finally she glanced through her tears and recognized the shirt and pants and she identified her father by his hand, one finger was missing.

Elizabeth was trembling but looked at the remains without showing the least emotion, she raised her hand to her face as if to suppress any exhibition of her feelings and simply said that it was her husband.

Dowd then looked at the body and did so without wincing. He said he could not recognize either the body or the clothes, he had not seen Ward since seeing him alive in his house, he said. He claimed he knew nothing about the matter.

The coroner's jury was satisfied that it was the body of Thomas Ward and determined that death had been caused by a fracture of the skull. They then retired to the Ward home and heard the evidence of several witnesses.

Peter St. Peter, a fellow farmer at New River, told the coroner's inquest into Ward's death that he had seen him a fortnight earlier.

"I came here the day after I saw him and asked Mrs. Ward where her husband was. She said she did not know, as he got up that morning before she did and went away somewhere. About a month ago, Ward came to my house, crying, and said he saw Tommy Dowd hugging and kissing his wife, and said that a man who would do that would do worse."

Mary Matthews also gave sworn testimony to the same effect, "Mr. Ward told me, a short time ago, that he saw Mrs. Ward get out of her bed and go to Dowd's bed and put her arms around his neck and kiss him. He also said there was no one on his side at the house but McCarthy and he did not dare to say a word.

"He said he lost his first wife this way and would probably lose this one also. He stated that he was afraid to turn Dowd out of his house as his wife would turn on him and make him 'turn McCarthy off.' I told him, 'If you want help you can get it'."

Ward did indeed have another wife ... and he was still legally married to her.

Although from Charlotte County, Thomas Ward had been the stagecoach driver between St. George and St. John. His first wife, Ann Ward, still lived in St. John in the Ingraham house on Sheffield Street. She told a *St. John Globe* reporter that she was a married woman and that her husband had deserted her "the year of the cholera."

She wouldn't discuss the cause of the separation and could not say positively whether or not the murdered Thomas Edward Ward was her husband, although she acknowledged that the name was the same and admitted she heard he had married again and was living at Magaguadavic. A married daughter offered the same story.

Elizabeth Ward, described as a "little woman, thin and careworn with a mild eye and soft voice" was originally Elizabeth Summers from Digdeguash, near St. Andrews. She and Thomas Ward were married in St. Stephen in 1859. They were reputed to have nine children but their 17 year-old daughter Annie and four year-old Susan were the only ones to share the rented one-and one-half-storey, five room McGowan house at New River during the 10 years before Ward disappeared from his home on the fateful Monday, September 9.

Later evidence, heard at the inquest indicated that the weekend before Ward disappeared had been a fractious affair. Generally a placid man Thomas Ward first accused David McCarthy of seducing his daughter, Annie, and ordered him to leave immediately. He told Annie to get out and never return then turned his wrath on Thomas Dowd and told him he would have to find another place to live.

Dowd was in custody at a hotel in Lepreaux and Elizabeth Ward was under house arrest for the murder of her husband on September 9. The inquest heard a variety of evidence, some of it conflicting, that suggested that any one of the household had reason to want to be rid of Thomas Ward. Evidence indicated that at one time he had simply disappeared for nearly three months before contacting Mrs. Ward from Halifax. Mrs. Ward simply presumed, she said, that her husband had gone away again.

On September 29 the coroner's jury found that Thomas Ward had come to his death at the hands of Thomas Dowd and that Elizabeth Ward was an accomplice to the murder.

Both Dowd and Elizabeth were taken to St. Andrews to await trial. Thomas Dowd was housed in the county jail and Elizabeth and four-year-old Susan landed in the debtor's cell.

Trial opened on November 15, 1878 before Mr. Justice Weldon at St. Andrews. Neither Dowd nor Elizabeth had counsel, conveniently all available lawyers were out of town at the time. The case was, of course, considered to be a hopeless one to defend.

By this time Dowd had changed his story, admitting that he had, indeed, killed Thomas Ward but that he had acted in self-defence. That Ward had attacked him on the fateful Monday morning when they met to begin work on the bridge and the haying. But he insisted that Mrs. Ward knew nothing of the murder, that he alone was responsible.

They did not believe Dowd, nor did they believe Elizabeth Ward when she claimed to know nothing of the affair. The focus of the Crown was, of course, the suspicions that Dowd and Elizabeth were lovers and that Elizabeth had lied when she told Mrs. Taylor on Monday morning that he had gone away, yet conceded that she did not miss him until supper time that day.

Both were found guilty and no recommendation was put forward in either case and they were sentenced to be hanged on January 14, 1879.

The St. Croix Courier took the county's legal representatives severely to task for their disappearance during the trial and, once the trial was over, the lawyers returned and mounted a strong campaign to spare the life of Elizabeth Ward. Petitions found their way to the Secretary of State and, in a precedent setting move, her death sentence was commuted but no new sentence was offered.

Thomas Dowd went to his death in a stoic and religious manner, accepting his fate but stressing his innocence. Innocence of both intentional murder of Thomas Ward and innocent of any intimacy with Elizabeth Ward.

"I never had any improper intimacy with Mrs. Ward and never knew her as a man or a woman except by her

The Gallows of New Brunswick

Thomas Dowd still protested his innocence of the murder of
Thomas Ward on the day he met the hangman
and thence to his grave.

clothing."

Dowd said he had made his confession both to the
Sheriff and to the priests who attended him and that he
had given them his permission to make those confessions
public.

"They do not differ from what I have said here."

The Gallows of New Brunswick

Dowd's innocence was believed by many, nevertheless on January 14 he went to his death through the method commonly referred to as "being jerked to eternity."

The procession was led by the Sheriff with Father Doyle bearing the crucifix and with Dowd on his left holding in his left hand a blessed candle. On arrival at the scaffold the priest and the prisoner knelt in prayer, Dowd kissed the wounds on the crucifix five times and then said that he was very thankful to the Sheriff and to the Jailer. He even blessed the people of St. Andrews and wished them well.

The scaffold was constructed in such a manner that, when the rope was cut, the body was jerked into the air and death, as it was afterwards ascertained by the jail physician, was instantaneous.

As the noose was placed around his neck and the black hood affixed to his head the bells of St. Andrews began to peal and, after the execution, the traditional black flag was raised above the jail.

He claimed his uncle made him do it

At the Westmorland Circuit Court in July of 1864 an action of trespass was tried, with William Hill as plaintiff and Zacariah Tingley as defendant. The facts of this action were brought to the attention of readers of the *Saint John Freeman* on the eve of the execution of Amos Hicks for the murder of the same William Hill named above. The information was presumed to be in the "best interests" of society so they might "more fully understand the story behind the recent tragedy (the killing of Hill on the Wednesday prior to this action of trespass brought by some members of the community) in the Dorchester-Sackville area of the province."

The facts of the case, as they were presented in evidence, included 1: the results of the lawsuit brought by Hill against Tingley, prior to Hill's death and 2: the relationship between Amos Hicks, who shot Hill, and the same Zacariah Tingley who the courts had found against in Hill's lawsuit.

In the July action of trespass the court was told that Hill, who was a poor man, had moved to a lot on wilderness land belonging to Tingley and built a small log house on it. In his suit, against Tingley, Hill swore that he did so under a verbal agreement with Tingley that the latter, who claimed a large extent of woodland in that neighbourhood, was to give him a Deed of the lot in consideration of his protecting the rest from plunderers.

Hill further contended that Tingley expressly directed him where to place the house and repeatedly urged him to commence its erection and made no objection to it until it was nearly completed.

When the house was finished Hill and his family , a wife and several children, moved into it. Then Tingley, along with five or six men, came to the house when Hill was not there and drove out the woman and children and totally demolished the house and most of the furniture in it.

Tingley denied having given Hill permission to go on the land or to build the house and the Chief Justice directed the jury that Hill had no legal title to do either but that Tingley was liable for any unnecessary damage done. The jury gave the latter a verdict for the full value of the articles destroyed or injured.

The land in question forms part of a very large body of wilderness land known in Westmorland as "The Sackville Rights" to most of which a title could only be obtained by priority of possession in the claimant, or those under whom he claims.

After the demolition of his house and the successful judgement against Tingley, Hill bought the "Rights" of certain parties in Sackville and claimed to be now entitled to the original lot by a title superior to Tingley's. He declared his determination to resume possession of the land and rebuild his house. It was during the prosecution of that determination that he was engaged in cleaning up the land near the former site, when he met his death.

Amos Hicks was Tingley's nephew and lived with him for some time working as a labourer on the property.

Hill was a man of great determination of character but was "inoffensive, honest and industrious and died in the assertion of what he doubtless believed to be his right, although strongly advised by his family and professional advisers not to persist in the conflict with Tingley," according to the writer of the story in the *Freeman*, who identified himself only as "L." He went on to say that Hill's remains "were followed to the grave yesterday by a long procession of all ranks in the community among whom but one feeling prevailed, that of sympathy for Hill's afflicted wife and children and of horror of the foul crime that had so cruelly deprived them of husband and father."

The murder was committed in Sackville but so near to the line between that parish and Dorchester that the spot is generally mentioned as being in Dorchester. According to evidence presented at the inquest Amos Hicks was of simple nature and, on hearing his uncle ranting against Hill, felt he was being called upon to do something about the situation.

He took his gun and made his way through the woods to where Hill was working and, in a friendly manner, asked the man if he was Mr. Hill and if he was working on building his house. Hill confirmed both statements and Hicks told him he was doing some hunting, with which statement he turned away and walked a few yards before turning and, taking careful aim, shooting Hill.

Hicks then proceeded to walk towards the village of Sackville and the residence of another relative.

After the inquest it was also learned that, as Hicks fled from Tingley's towards the village of Sackville, he met a person who knew him. Hicks told him that he had shot and wounded old Hill. He then requested him, if he met anyone in pursuit of him to send them on the wrong scent.

Hicks was found guilty of killing Hill and was hanged at Dorchester at 9:30 a.m. on September 8, 1864. The *Freeman's* telegraphic advances said that a large gathering ,of people both male and female, was present to witness the "hapless murderer" paying the penalty of his crime.

Two baptist ministers followed him to the gallows and read his confession of the murder. To the last the murderer implicated Tingley as being the instigator of the deed for which he was now about to suffer the punishment prescribed by law.

Prior to the hanging it was speculated that the Lieutenant-Governor might commute the sentence. The *Free-*

man notes "The case undoubtedly gave His Excellency a good deal of concern, but as there were really no extenuating circumstances he could not justly interfere.

'God will take care of that'

In the eyes of the press of the time Angele Poulin may have been "unprepossessing" at best and "repulsive" at worst but in the eyes of the two men in her life she was an attractive and desirable woman. She married Xavier Poulin late in life according to 1850s standards, she was 23 at the time, and she bore him eight children before he became ill in 1864.

Leprosy was a fairly common illness in the northeastern part of New Brunswick in the last half of the nineteenth century and Xavier was diagnosed as having this malignant and debilitating disease. Moreover, he was forbidden by his parish priest to have intercourse with his wife.

Angele was born into poverty and ignorance, Xavier was a back-woodsman, a woodcutter by trade. As his illness worsened he was less and less able to work and provide for his family and eventually they became wards of the parish.

Oliver Gallien, a 25 year-old man as poverty-stricken as the Poulins, nevertheless befriended them and the entire family moved into his one-room cabin on Caraquet Island.

Husky, dark-faced Gallien fathered Angele's next two children over the following 10 years of misery for Xavier Poulin, whose body was covered with sores. He was frequently confined to bed in abject pain. Yet, surprisingly, in the Spring of 1874 Xavier's condition began to improve. Soon he was moving from bed to a chair and then he was walking with the aid of a stick. He began to go for short walks in the woods and to chop wood.

Angele was by then pregnant with Gallien's third child. She had been agitating him for the past two years to kill her husband, now with Xavier's health improving Angele became even more persistent. Even in front of visitors she would urge Oliver to kill him. At one time she openly debated the merits of a knife, blows to the head or strangulation, an option she believed might be considered a natural death.

Gallien regularly demurred, pleading lack of heart for the job. Xavier, apparently, was aware of Angele's plotting.

On April 20, when Gallien's sister was visiting them, Xavier took his axe and went to the woods around ten o'clock in the morning. Gallien left about an hour later, he came back and talked to Angele outside in the yard then returned to the woods again for half an hour.

When he returned the second time Angele went to the woods and she, too, returned in half an hour at which time Gallien washed himself and changed his clothes. Angele threw the clothes in the loft of the cabin and proceeded to continue her visit with Delina Gallien.

By four o'clock Delina wondered where Xavier was, Angele gave her directions and she set out to the woods to find him. It was not too long before she raised the alarm, Xavier was lying dead in an open clearing, it looked as if he had been hit on the head with an axe but Delina could not find one anywhere near.

Gallien was distressed with the news but Angele was her usual, easy-going self.

Gallien and a neighbour went to get the body and brought it to the cabin in a cart where Angele washed the blood off and tied a white bandanna around Xavier's head to hide the wounds.

Gallien kept protesting that he had not killed him.

The inquest, held two days later, attached no blame but the next day Gallien went to the magistrate and confessed, in front of witnesses, that he had killed Xavier. He said he killed him with a stick and his fists, not with an axe and he claimed that Angele had nagged him into committing the murder.

The medical evidence did not agree with Gallien's confession but indicated that the fatal wound might have been made with the blunt edge of an axe.

Gallien was put in jail in Bathurst to await trial, frequently telling any who would listen that Angele had been after him for two years to kill Xavier and that she warned him if he didn't do it, she would.

He also said that when he left, after beating Xavier, the 60 year-old man was alive and trying to crawl.

Angele was arrested and charged with the murder of her husband. The police believed that when Gallien returned from beating Xavier, Angele went to the woods and finished the job. This was what they believed but they couldn't prove it.

Gallien's one-day trial was held in Bathurst September 3. Mr. Justice J.W. Weldon presided and F.W. Morrison was Crown Prosecutor. J.S. Barbie acted in defence of Oliver Gallien but was unable to present any witnesses or evidence that might lessen his guilt.

It only took 20 minutes for the jury reach a verdict of guilty but they recommended mercy because Gallien had confessed and had said he was sorry.

Angele was next, she was charged with being an accessory before the fact and the same evidence which convicted her lover was presented by the same attorneys before the same judge and heard by the same jury but with one exception, Oliver Gallien was called to testify against her.

His evidence was simple.

"I don't know," he said when questioned.

"I can't remember," he said.

The judge later suggested that Angele's influence over him was apparently as strong as ever.

The jury took an hour to deliberate but they came

back with a verdict of guilty ...... with no recommendation for mercy.

Both Angele and Oliver were sentenced to death. Oliver to be executed in Bathurst on October 29, Angele, because she was pregnant, was given a reprieve until January 5, 1875.

To the amazement of reporters in attendance neither prisoner showed any reaction to the sentence. It was some time before they learned the reason for this.

The judge had delivered the sentence in English, the interpreter was so awed by the occasion that he forgot to translate it into French. As a result, both Oliver and Angele were led from the courtroom ignorant of their fate because neither could speak English.

Several hours later someone realized what had happened and translated the sentence.

In Oliver Gallien's case Judge Weldon was adamant that he could see nothing in the evidence or the conduct of the prisoner that would warrant mercy. He said he believed that of the two, however, Angele was the more guilty.

On October 29 1874, Gallien was hanged in a special enclosure built outside the front wall of the prison. As he was led to the gallows Angele's face wore an unrevealing mask but, later, when his body was removed from the prison for burial she broke down and cried.

It was the only expression of emotion her jailers noted on their records.

Strangely enough Angele's sentence was commuted on December 22 to life in Dorchester Penitentiary where she remained for the next ten and one half years. In 1885 it was decided that all female federal prisoners were to be sent to Kingston Penitentiary but the warden at Dorchester suggested that Angele should be pardoned.

The Minister contacted Judge Weldon who obviously failed to remember his comment at the time of the trial. He agreed to the commuting of the sentence, even offering the comment that she appeared to be "a poor, halfwitted person." In fact he added that if the law had permitted it he would have imposed a lesser penalty on her ten years earlier!

On June 29, 1885 Angele Poulin was pardoned into the care of one of her married daughters. One wonders if she remembered Oliver Gallien's words when, the day before he was to hang he was permitted a short meeting with her. Angele asked him if he forgave her for involving him in the crime.

"God will take care of that," he replied.

I'm Murdered! said Joe Steadman ... and he was

The courthouse was jammed to the rafters on August 2, 1892 when Justice Wortman opened the Coroner's inquest into the Aug. 1 shooting death of Moncton policeman Joseph Steadman.

The coroner's jury, E.C. Cole, foreman; J.W. Oulton, George McSweeney, F. Girvan, H.D. Chapman, G.R. Sangster and James Doyle, empanelled for the occasion, were sworn in then left the court to view the body of Joseph Steadman before proceeding with the business of the day.

No attorney appeared for the Crown, this was deemed not to be necessary under the existing circumstance. D. Grant appeared for the defendant, known at that time as "Buck Whalen."

The second man, believed to be involved in the robbery and possibly Steadman's death, known only as "Jim," was still at large.

The court session began with Marshal Charles Foster describing the circumstances under which the Steadman death occurred. He told the jury that the situation developed following receipt of a telegram from Chatham advising him of a robbery committed therein which some Mexican coin was stolen. A later telegram said the money taken from the safe was in one, two, and five dollar bills, a few American fives, about $70 in currency; also about $50 in old silver, mostly Mexican dollars with some French five franc pieces. There was also a quantity of doubloons worth about four duena.

Foster said he knew between two and four o'clock the day before the shooting that there were "suspicious characters" at the Donnelly house on Telegraph Street, but at that time he didn't believe he had any authority to arrest them. His instructions came at six o'clock, after further telegrams from W. Wilson in Chatham described the "suspicious parties," as "one being tall with a slight moustache and bad looking, the other was short, wearing brown clothes and a cap and had not shaved for a day or two."

By then the men had left the Donnelly house for Salisbury but, sometime after eight o'clock, Foster got word they had returned and the following scenario began to unfold.

"I proceeded to Mrs. Donnelly's house and took three officers with me, policemen Scott and Steadman, constable Colburn and a man named McFee.

"When I arrived there I took the front door and instructed the officers to take the different position. Policeman Steadman followed me to the front door. I stopped to take out my revolver and he said 'Marshal, I'll go around with the others.'

"I went in the door immediately ... I instructed the men to make the arrest under my authority. I heard a woman say 'Here is Marshal Foster.' I saw a man go into the next room and slam the door after him. I gave chase through the door then I heard the shooting. I ran back and out the front door and saw Steadman falling down, he made the remark, 'I'm murdered'."

Constable Charles Colburn said he had gone around to the back of the Telegraph Street house and saw Joe Steadman on the south side. "I was about 20 feet back from the street. I saw the deceased come to the door. When I saw him he had hold of the prisoner (Buck Whalen) with the right hand and was hitting him with his baton with his left. When I first heard the shooting I was on the north side near the window and I then ran around to the south side. When I arrived there Steadman was striking him.

"After a short time the prisoner fired one shot and as

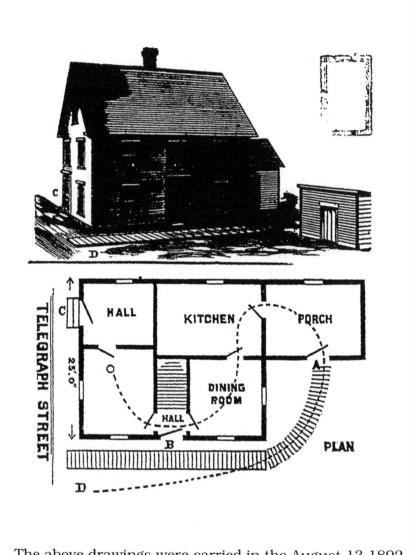

The above drawings were carried in the August 13, 1892 issue of *The Progress* and heralded as "The spot made memorable by the Moncton murder. Sketches which are of interest now and will be of value to the future."

near as I could see he had his hand in close proximity to the person of the deceased. Altogether I thought I heard five shots, the first four shots went off very suddenly but there was some stop between the first four and the last. I think the last shot was the one that proved fatal as they both fell immediately after the report."

The coroner's jury pulled minute details of the incident both from those involved and from witnesses such as Seymour Gould who said he followed the officers up the street and was standing in the centre of the street, opposite the alley where the action took place. He apparently assisted in carrying Steadman to the Park Hotel and testified that he was dead when they got him there.

Another observer, who heard six shots, said he had the impression the shots came from "east" of the two men. He said, "I first saw a man come out of the side door and clinch with the deceased. I think deceased used his baton when clinched and struck at him. I then heard a shot and in a very short period I heard a second; then there were four shots in rapid succession. The four shots appeared to be to the eastward of them. I didn't see who fired these four shots. I saw those two men come towards the street and the deceased hit and stunned him. I saw Mr. Scott strike the prisoner and heard Mr. Steadman say, 'My God. I'm murdered'.

"I was close enough to see only the two men when I first heard the shot. The man they arrested was continually under my eye from the time he met Steadman at the door until he was arrested. I could not tell the position the pistol was held when the first shot was fired. The deceased fell in the road after the four shots were fired."

Scott, the second Moncton policeman, said he did not see the prisoner holding a gun but that he had seen flashes from a pistol. What he did see was fellow policeman Steadman struggling with Buck and hitting him with his baton. Scott added his baton to the struggle from behind, following the two men as they made their way to the street where he put handcuffs on Buck when they fell. It was not until then that he realized Steadman had been shot.

"I saw no revolver in the prisoner's hands," he said. "I fired no shot myself."

Maggie Donnelly said a couple of strangers came to the house the previous Saturday . She said the men were in the dining room when the marshal entered the house. When her sister remarked that Marshal Foster had come in the two men ran to the back of the house and the marshal ran after them. She heard two shots fired but could not see the flash.

"From what I heard the fellow say, I was of the opinion that they had something hid that they wanted to go after. They both got new caps yesterday. My brother bought them for them, they gave him the money.

"There was a man playing the organ when the marshal came in but he left our house when the shots went off."

Selina Donnelly, Maggie's sister, said she remembered the marshal coming to the door at nine o'clock. "I heard the first bell ring and, upon going to the door, met the marshal. I went to the dining room door and said, 'The cops is about the house.'

"I had no special object in saying it ... when I made this remark Buck put his hand in his pocket and held up his hand and called Jim ... I suppose it was a revolver that was in his hand. He then made for the door."

Selina Donnelly went on to say that the two men had come to the door the previous Saturday morning in a covered carriage but that they had no baggage.

After her testimony the coroner's jury interviewed witnesses regarding the disappearance of the second suspect in the Chatham robbery named "Jim," who escaped capture at the Donnelly house the previous day.

The Gallows of New Brunswick

Testimony to the fact that a man dressed in black, wearing a black cap and a striped necktie was seen in Salisbury "acting strangely" was presented by W. Mullins an area farmer. His evidence, although second hand, was deemed by the court to be highly descriptive of the missing "Jim" who, according to "the little Donnelly girl" was indeed wearing a striped necktie.

The first sighting of "Jim" was by John Corbett, a railroad section man for the area between Moncton and Boundary Creek. A second sighting was reported coming in from George Wilmot, the section foreman for the same area. According to *The Daily Transcript* of Tuesday, August 2, "the news has caused intense excitement and the line is now carefully watched and every train hand is on the lookout."

In the meantime the same paper informed its readers that the prisoner, known as "Buck" had been quite ill the morning of the inquest and had "positively declined to give his name, home or anything that would lead to his identity."

A former marshal, Ferdinand Thibodeau visited Buck in his cell and questioned him. Thibodeau said he was sure he knew the man from a burglary four years earlier. He said he chased him until the man entered the woods and escaped. However, after questioning Buck, Thibodeau could not be positive that it was the same man and was unable to offer an identity.

There was considerable evidence presented indicating the eager interest of "Buck" and "Jim," who claimed to be sailors, in the contents of the daily papers as they became available. Discussions regarding the accuracy of robbery accounts in the papers were overheard by the Donnellys, who admitted to having known "Buck" for some time.

The men told the Donnellys they were going "away" on the CPR but the man "Jim" who Mrs. Donnelly described as "the dark one," went out and, when he returned, told Buck that his "clothes were not done" and that they were late for the train.

69

Further evidence placed a revolver firmly in the hands of "Buck" at the time he was informed by Selina Donnelly that the "cops" were in the house.

The next day "Jim" was still at large and a $500 reward was put up by the provincial government and a $250 reward was posted by the City of Moncton for evidence leading to his arrest.

In the meantime the coroner's inquest continued and, after the medical report from Dr. O.J. McCully, found that on Aug. 1,1892 Joseph E. Steadman, while in the discharge of his duty as police officer ...... "came to his death by a shot from a revolver in the hands of a person to us unknown, called Buck, who is now in custody, and that he fired the said shot with intent to kill and murder the said Joseph E. Steadman."

Still under the jurisdiction of "Stipendiary" Wortman a Preliminary Trial opened immediately. An important piece of evidence given by Scott, the other Moncton policeman involved would, in today's courts, weigh heavily in favour of the accused.

According to the *Transcript*, Scott repeated his earlier testimony that "The person now in court is the man deceased had hold of. I ran to them and struck the prisoner with my baton. The blow apparently staggered the prisoner and they rushed off the sidewalk to the street. I struck again and he fell about the middle of the street. I seen no person come out the back door of the house as I ran around where the prisoner fell. I put the handcuffs on him as quick as I could. I heard deceased say, 'My God. I'm murdered'."

Evidence immediately following Scott's was given by eye-witness Charles Coburn, who testified to watching the struggle between Steadman and Buck and to the fact that there had been at least four shots fired in quick succession, then two others after about four or five seconds.

"I was by the window on the north side when those shots were fired. I heard no other until I got near the southwest corner and came around the southwest corner. I heard the last shot. Mr. Scott struck the prisoner and he fell. The deceased then dropped, but straightened up then put up his hands and exclaimed, 'My God, I'm murdered.' They would be on the street. I saw no person standing in the alley except the deceased, the prisoner and Scott."

Further evidence from Thomas Buckley who said that of the "five or six shots" he heard all did not come from the direction of where the prisoner and Steadman were "clinched."

As the trial progressed reports of Jim being sighted in a variety of locations continued and "Buck" finally identified himself as being Robert Olsen, an American "of Scandinavian origin."

So concerned were the authorities with this man's threat to the community that seven armed men were set to guard the lockup. But the talk of the town was the mystery woman from Sackville and Jim's supposedly having left a horse and buggy, prepaid, at the International Hotel and scheduled to be taken to Bangor, Maine.

Rumours ran rampant

On Thursday, August 4, a woman and a little boy of about 11 years of age made their appearance in Moncton and registered at the Queen hotel as Mrs. Griffin and son of Sackville.Ex Marshal Thibodeau is said to have recognized her as being the wife of a well known thimble pen faker. Someone, the *Transcript* writer suggests it must have been a spiritualist, managed to get a peek into the box carried by the woman and placed under the seat of the aforementioned buggy. In it were a bottle of liniment, a small quantity of white lead – and several wigs and a false moustache.

It was noted that although the items appeared suspicious the woman was allowed to go on her way to Bangor.

Red herrings appeared to be the order of the day on

Thursday which saw four men "armed to the teeth" marching to the Donnelly house where they surrounded the premises. They had been informed that a suspicious looking man had gone in the house. They caught a man named Dryden and proceeded to march him off to the lockup. After giving a satisfactory account of himself he was allowed to leave, no doubt making a hasty exit of the town!

Stories and reports reached a peak with the news that the elusive Jim had indeed been captured in Salisbury and would be arriving on the freight train due to arrive at 9:45 Thursday morning. The news spread like wildfire. Merchants closed their stores and workmen in their shops laid down their tools and ran to the station, about 500 people, including men, women and children, congregated eager to have a look at the noted desperado.

The train arrived ... but no "Jim."

The crowd gave voice to their displeasure.

During the trial on Friday, August 5 Frederick Barker, a Fredericton native who was on Telegraph Street on Sunday night in the company of Thomas Buckley testified to the number of shots, the fact that several appeared to come from a distance away from "Buck" and Steadman. He also testified that it was after Scott hit "Buck" with his baton that he heard Steadman's now famous statement: "My God, I'm murdered."

At nine o'clock Saturday morning, August 6 the evidence against "Buck," now known as Robert Olsen, was reviewed and he was charged with the murder of Moncton policeman Joe Steadman. He returned a plea of "Not Guilty" and was subsequently committed to incarceration in the Dorchester jail until the time of his trial.

Buck claimed he first met his pal Jim about three weeks previous to Sunday night's events. This is seen to bear out the theory of a Detective Gross of Montreal who believed he was the same Buck Whalen he knew in Montreal who had recently finished serving a term in the Vermont state prison. Speculation was that Buck may have been serving that sentence since the former Moncton Marshal Thibodeau lost him in woods near Moncton four years earlier.

In the process of trying to get Buck to sign his name or make his mark, a prison official began to get more and more frustrated and suspicious. When he was asked how he spelled his name he replied that he couldn't spell. The next day, when asked to sign his name, he told them he could write but the handcuffs prevented him from doing so. They strongly believed that Buck was still "Buck," an unknown.

It appeared that in June of 1892 he had been in Moncton and had ordered a coat and vest at W.E. Bishop's tailor shop, using the name of James Murphy and claiming he had run away from a ship in St. John. At that time he told the tailor he had come from the United States where he worked in Lowell, Mass.

According to the St. John *Progress*, Buck's treatment while under arrest was not in keeping with "common humanity."

His wounds were not attended to and he was made to feel that he was in custody to suffer all that he can legally be made to suffer. In its search for the truth of such allegations the *Progress* correspondent visited Buck in jail. The following is his report:

To the unbiased and receptive mind this is the picture he presented.

A rather small, fair man, who might have been anywhere between 30 and 40, or even younger, so baffling is a fair complexion where age is concerned, lying wearily on his cot, with the oilcloth cushion of a chair doubled up under his head for a pillow, manacled hands and singularly small feet. He looked pale and ill, but on being told that someone had come to see him, moved stiffly to his feet and sat up civilly to be looked at and questioned.

The Gallows of New Brunswick

The above photograph was carried in the August 6, 1892 issue of the *Progress*. The caption notes "Olsen in his cell objects to being photographed."

He had been removed from the dark cell and occupied the last of a row of grated cells. Seen in the morning light, his face could scarcely be termed prepossessing, but few men look well with three weeks growth of beard on their faces and a bruise on their forehead, and this man was no worse looking than scores of others one meets every day on the street .... except that he looked as if he had recently recovered from a bad spree and was still feeling the effects. So far from looking like a desperado, his face wore a mingled expression of fright and patience, and he seemed so broken down and tired that the writer mercifully cut the interview short.

...... his head pained him a good deal and his leg, he said, was very bad, "it is so feverish."

It had only been dressed once and had been bleeding a good deal since then.

When asked if they were treating him well, Buck replied "No, not very well." Then hastily added "as well as I can expect I suppose."

At the close of the conversation the prisoner limped painfully back to his cot. His left ankle was quite swollen from the wound in his leg, and he seemed to be suffering a great deal, "yet in double-dyed Christian ... Moncton, his wound had only been dressed once.

He is a criminal. Possibly a murderer but still common humanity would suggest that he should receive ordinary care.

The description of Jim was now running daily in newspapers throughout the province, along with the rewards offered. As a result many a tramp or other seemingly suspicious character was arrested and questioned, then let go.

The infamous Jim was still at large when the date of Sept. 13, 1892 was set for the Grand Jury to hear the evidence against he and the man known as Buck Whalen.

The search for Buck's elusive buddy, "Jim"

Jim was said to be:

Of middle age, probably 30, about five feet-two inches in height, dressed in black clothes, dark shirt, wore a necktie with black spots, whiskers three or four weeks' growth and had no hat on when escaped.

This is slightly different from the earlier version released immediately after the arrest of Buck and, when the rumour arose in the streets of Moncton on Friday evening, August 12, 1892 that Jim had not only been captured but was actually coming on the evening train, the majority of the citizens received the information with a cynical smile.

"I think I have heard something like that before," was the general opinion according to an eyewitness account by Geoffrey Cuthbert Strange, writing in the St. John *Progress.*

They had heard it before, and so many times that the news had lost all its former piquancy –like champagne which has been left uncorked, the sparkle had gone off and left it flat and stale

Indeed there had been so many suppositions of "Jims" sighted in the offing lately that the experienced citizen, who had already had one or two fruitless runs to the station in the hope of seeing the long expected and anxiously sought "Jim," requires some stronger confirmation of the report than mere rumours. But for once rumour was correct and the one and only original Jim was really on the nine o'clock freight train en route for Moncton.

The Gallows of New Brunswick

When this became known, beyond all possibility of doubt, about one-half of the population resolved themselves into a reception committee and started for the station.

The rain was coming down in torrents, but it would have taken a cloud burst apparently to dampen the enthusiasm of the crowd; even the "gentle sex" was well represented, the fair ones donning water proofs and rubbers and joining in the procession with an order born of that love of sport which is said to be implanted in the breast of every true born Briton and by the time the "number 38" steamed into the station there was scarcely standing room on the wet, slippery platform.

As the involuntary hero of the occasion was assisted from the car there was a frantic rush on the part of the crowd to get a look at him; people elbowed their dearest friends and relentlessly trampled on the toes of their nearest relations in their mad efforts to catch a glimpse of the small, frightened looking man whose head was bound up and whose face showed most unpleasant evidence of its contact with the brawny knuckles of ex-policeman Peter Carroll of Pictou: "and, by the way," Strange said, "I believe the said knuckles suffered only in a secondary degree from their contact with Jim's head."

Some of the crowd were disappointed however, as the train was stopped at the northern crossing and the prisoner walked down to the cab stand and hurried into a cab.

As the cab drove off the excitement passed all bounds and yells of "Hurrah for Jim!" "Hurrah for Jim!" "Hurrah for Jim!" rent the murky air. Boys climbed up on the cab and hung on behind shouting frantically, only to be slashed at with the whip and, after a moment's discouragement, to seize upon a fresh hold and cling with renewed energy to Jim's chariot wheels.

The procession down Main Street was almost a triumphal march, and by the time the police station was reached it had augmented to such an extent that neither

77

circus day in a country town, nor the orange procession on the twelth could be compared with it; everybody was there and everybody felt it incumbent upon them to announce their presence by vigorous shouting, so that by the time the prisoner and his guard reached the lockup the surging shouting crowd looked so formidable that the prisoner is said to have expressed a fear of lynching, and begged the police to protect him.

Once inside the gaol, he was handed over to the kind administrations of Dr. Botsford, who dressed his wounded head, and prescribed liberal doses of beef tea to be fed through the night to the famished creature who had been without food for eight days, except for the few berries he picked in the woods.

...... It was late into the night before the last excited citizen had departed, and a sort of watchful and open-eyed peace settled down over the city.

Strange goes on to laud the care accorded Jim by Dr. Botsford, in comparison to the treatment accorded Buck. He also deplored the fact that, although everyone was relieved at the final capture of Jim, so much capital, $750 reward, is going out of the province.

A following column, unsigned, appears to carry the flavour of Strange's writing. Some excerpts are repeated here and colourfully reflect the mood of the area in terms both of the capture and of the skills of the Moncton police force of the time:

Now that the game is over the question of prizes is the next one to be considered, and as the spoils belong legally to the victor there can be no doubt that the great cash prize in the game of chance has been won by a stranger, a man who had a narrow escape from being a member of the Moncton police force, and who has satisfactorily proved what a great mistake "the powers that be made" in not securing his services.

"Our own police force have undoubtedly done their

best and the special constables sworn in since the search began have not been behind hand in doing their duty and following up the many and varied trails on which they have started but luck has been against them and, where they failed. Mr. Peter O. Carroll of Pictou, has succeeded and fairly won the coveted reward of $750.

"Public sentiment seems to be unanimous upon one point, best expressed in a very few words, namely – Three cheers for Peter Carroll!"

And what of Jim?

He, whose proper name was James Willis, would be tried before the Grand Jury along with his friend Buck.

Part Two

The Trial

Grand Jury: Court opened at 2 p.m. September 13, Judge Fraser presiding; Attorney General Blair and Hon. Henry R. Emmerson for the Crown; David Grant and R.E. Smith for the defense.

Jury included W.F. George, foreman; Hiram W. Palmer, J.W. McManus, William Ogden, J.F. Sherry; C.A. Gilbert, H.R. Fawcett, G.F. Atkinson, Alex Girvan, J.M. Wallace, Andrew Jones, William Humphrey, E. Goodwin, Arthur Snowdeen, N. Miner, S.L. Chapman, J.J. McGrath, J. McNaughton, N. Dudscot, J.D. Weldon, A. Webster, James Anderson.

The Grand Jury, primarily reviewing the evidence submitted to the coroner's jury found True Bills against both Buck and Jim and a new jury for the trial of Buck on the charge of murder was called immediately.

David Grant, Buck's solicitor immediately challenged the jurors on the grounds that they had already heard the evidence and formed an opinion. W. Cochrane and J. Hazen Copp were then named "triers" who would query the prospective jurors.

The first juror was found to be a fellow member of the dead policeman's Orange Lodge. He was queried as to whether he had read a newspaper or formed an opinion in the case. The triers obviously were persuaded that he had not formed an opinion and deemed him qualified to sit on the jury. A similarly just trial was given subsequent jurors, eight of whom were challenged by the defence and two by the Crown. The following were selected:

M.B. Palmer, Charles Crowman, Philip F.Gotre, all

of Dorchester; W. Milner, Wood Point, Sackville, John B. Thompson, Moncton, J.N. Evans, Sackville, Cent Sullivan, Irishtown, Albert Avard, Pt. du Batt, Henry S. Cripps, Petitcodiac, Izey Avard, Bristol, L.W. McAnn, Moncton, John Johnson, Grand Aunce.

Once again, with only a few exceptions, the same witnesses gave virtually the same testimony they had given during the coroner's inquest.

During the coroner's inquest both Moncton Policeman "Scott" and at least two other witnesses indicated that the probably fatal gunshot and "flash' were immediately preceded by Scott pounding the prisoner with his baton from behind. Scott himself, who was busily cuffing Buck, said that he did not know Steadman had been shot until the dying man said, "My God. I'm murdered."

According to the newspaper report later testimony as to when the fatal shot was fired in conjunction with Scott's supporting bludgeoning of the prisoner was less clear.

Two witnesses gave similar yet conflicting evidence as to remarks overheard in the jail during a conversation between Buck and Jim.

The second of these was from a young man called Henry Jones, a 16 year-old who worked in the jail. He is quoted as saying that, as he was sweeping the hall near the cells of the two men on Tuesday morning, August 23 he heard Buck talking of the shooting. Jones said Buck told Jim he had "almost cried after hearing how good a man the deceased officer was," and said, "My God I am sorry I shot him now."

Jones said Buck told Jim he could not help it, that he went to point his revolver to fire at which point someone hit him on the head, which made him drop the revolver "quite a piece." He intended to raise his revolver again and shoot over "his," presumably Steadman's, shoulder but he got another clout over the head just as he was going to pull the trigger, which lowered the revolver which then shot

Steadman.

This evidence supposedly substantiated that given by Peter O. Carroll, the man who successfully captured the elusive Jim and who was placed nearby Buck's and Jim's cells in order to eavesdrop on their conversations. Carroll subsequently told the court a story similar to that of the young jail worker, to the effect that the fatal shot and the bludgeoning of Buck by Scott happened almost instantaneously: The only variation to the story was that he claimed Buck told Jim that he intentionally shot Steadman and would have "got away" if Scott had not hit him on the head from behind.

Carroll's testimony was accepted by the court as being reliable and, "you know it's true" the Attorney General told the jury.

To the day of his death Buck maintained that Carroll lied but he never questioned or denied young Jones' testimony.

The court refused to accept a charge of manslaughter, which would appear today to be the proper charge. Certainly Buck's lawyer fought well for him and there was talk of appealing the murder verdict but nothing was done about it. The jury recommended mercy but Judge Fraser didn't appear to hear that recommendation. Buck, whose proper name is presumed to be Robert Olsen, was sentenced to hang.

Part Three
The hangman gets Buck's approval
... it's a ceremonial affair

Of all the research I have done for this book none has been more fascinating than the story of Robert Olsen, alias Buck Whalen. I applaud both the Moncton Transcript and the St. John Progress of 1892 and the journalists who covered Buck's and Jim's trials. Of particular fascination is the following detailed account of the day prior to and the day of Buck's hanging on December 1. **dd**

On Thursday, September 22, 1892 Judge Fraser passed the following sentence on Robert Olsen, alias "Buck:

The sentence of the court is that for the crime of the murder of Joseph E. Steadman in the city of Moncton on the first day of August that you, Robert Olsen, alias Buck, be conveyed back to the place from which you came and be safely kept until the first day of December in the year of our Lord ... 1892 to be then within the walls of the old jail hanged by the neck until you are dead. May God have mercy on your soul.

In the 69 days that followed this sentence Buck apparently spent a considerable amount of time with Father Cormier.

<u>November 30, the day before the hanging</u>.

On Wednesday afternoon, between two and three o'clock, Buck was taken from his cell by Deputy Sheriff Wilson and given his last recreation in a prolonged walk up and down the corridor.

Buck spoke freely but appeared to be quite concerned about the execution. He asked if the hangman had arrived. When answered in the affirmative he then asked if he had had much experience. He was told 'yes' again. Then he asked if it was the same man who had hanged "those people in Canada."

When he was told 'yes' he said, "I am glad they have an experienced man. I do not want to die by being slowly strangled to death."

Wednesday evening the low , sweet strains of two female voices sounded along the corridor from Buck's cell. First the voices appeared deeply affected and the notes subdued but soon they gathered confidence, force and volume and the sweet strains of *There's Life for a Look at the Crucified One*, *Mercy is Free*, and, *He gave His Life for Thee* rang as the sweetness of a bell through the prison.

According to *The Daily Transcript* it was one of the most touching episodes of the day and one "keenly appreciated by the condemned man."

The singers were Mrs. Harvey Atkinson and Mrs. H.R. Emmerson. Buck asked for Mrs. Atkinson and he also asked to see Mrs. Emmerson's little daughter, Ethel. He then asked the ladies to come the next morning and wish him farewell.

He said, "I am only just beginning to find out how kind people are, when I have to leave them."

It would seem that the personality of "Buck" had undergone a complete metamorphosis in the months since his sentence.

The singing was followed by some scripture readings and some advice from Father Cormier who told Buck not to assume the bravado of the world but "to imitate the patient walk of the Saviour who, without having done a single wrong, had gone to a more terrible death."

Mrs. Atkinson was interviewed by *The Transcript* following her conversation with Buck, during which she had asked him what she should tell the journalist when talking to him.

"He said, 'I wish you to state that standing right in the presence of death and knowing that I will stand before God in a few hours, that if I shot Steadman that night I did not know it."

Mrs. Atkinson also probed more into Buck's

background, questioning him on some of the statements he had made during the trial. Buck countered some lies he had spoken, specifically his age, which is thirty-three, not thirty (he was born in 1850, he said) and that he had lied when he told the sheriff his name was Robert Burke. (*There still appears to be a 10 year discrepancy in this information. The murder, the trial and the hanging all took place in year 1892.**dd**)

"He said his only brother was killed in the seven days Battle of the Wilderness. He had not seen his only sister for eighteen years, since she was married to a Mr. Burr Butler, a sporting man in Chicago whose father was one of the wealthiest men in Buffalo. After they were married Buck went away out West. He says he has been living among criminals ever since he was six years old."

Throughout their conversations Mrs. Atkinson was impressed with Buck's attitude and fully convinced that he had changed his ways. Knowing that she was a member of the Women's Christian Temperance Union (WCTU) and the King's Daughters he implored her to use her influence to see that homeless boys in Moncton were taken care of.

"Look after the boys," he implored her. "Remember the boys."

Buck had expressed similar feelings to Father Cormier who said he appeared convinced that if boys were given a good home they would not end up in a life of crime as he had done.

His request to see Jim was granted and the two men met for a lengthy talk. In the beginning they discussed religion and the importance of Buck being prepared for his death, then the conversation turned to Jim, who had been sentenced to a 25 year incarceration, and his future.

"I hear you are taking a painting course," Buck said. "Why didn't you go into the machine shop and learn a good trade."

Then, in a lower voice that could not be overheard very well Buck asked Jim if he ever heard news a 'particular person' was alive to tell them where his body was and "they will look after it: but it would be better if they were dead and then I will have no one to care for me."

He then implored Jim that "you must not go back to your old life. Your old associations were no good."

For awhile the men reminisced about some of the good times they had and even managed to laugh from time to time. Eventually Buck said he felt resigned to his fate and the conversation turned to newspaper reports and Buck inquired about Radcliffe, the hangman scheduled to preside at his execution the next day.

Jim said he hadn't seem him but knew he was "the same one who did the business for the fellows up in Ontario."

They then proceeded to discuss Radcliffe's qualifications and concluded that the man would indeed carry out the business properly.

"I would like to see the gallows," Buck said. "Just to see how it works. I am, you know, of a mechanical strain of mind myself."

"It's better for you not to think of that now," Jim said. " Better to think of your hereafter."

Buck suggested Jim should contact Mrs. Atkinson if he ever needed help. "She is a good woman and will be kind to you. She was very kind to me."

The warden then told Jim it was time to go.

"Give me your duke," Buck said and the men shook hands emotionally.

"In the morning, Buck, look from the window towards the penitentiary. In the third window on the second storey of the workshop you will see a red handkerchief in the window. That will be my last farewell to you.

"Goodbye. Brace up. Be of brave heart."

The two comrades in crime separated, never to meet again on earth.

Father Cormier, Roman Catholic priest at the penitentiary had been spiritual advisor to Buck from the time he was incarcerated and was deeply moved at his impending death.

"I really believe Buck has changed," he told *The Transcript*. " I told him that some good souls must have been praying for him fervently and that he had been abundantly blessed with the grace of God. I believe he is a thoroughly changed man – that he is repentant."

The priest went on to say that the visits of Mrs. Atkinson and her friends had a tremendous influence for good on him.

"He says he will die knowing he was innocent because he did not intend to fire the shot that killed Steadman, although he freely admits that his life has been a bad one – that he was a wicked man. ...

"He expresses no fear and says he is ready to die."

Earlier Buck had told Father Cormier that before he was "of the opinion that a man could (not) be happy unless he was gloriously drunk, but now I am perfectly happy."

The scaffold and gallows were erected just outside the building and a temporary shed built around them. About 50 persons were allowed to be present at the execution.

Mr. Humphrey Browser, under the direction of Radcliffe, the hangman, built the scaffold for the gallows that would hang Buck the next day. It consisted of two upright posts 18 feet four inches clear of the floor with a transverse beam. In the beam were two pulleys – one in the centre of the beam which would receive the rope attached to Buck's neck. The rope is run through the second pulley, which is outside the post that receives the rope attached to Buck's neck. The rope is run through the second pulley outside the post and is tied to the iron weight of 385 lbs. The weight is caught up to the beam and, when tripped, the weight falls, the prisoner is immediately jerked upwards and falls with a rebound but does not touch the floor.

Radcliffe explained that the knot of the noose is placed

in such a way that, unlike other gallows, the victim does not suffer a broken neck but dies almost instantly from the pressure of the impact.

The weight is attached to a trip and, when released, falls with a heavy thud into a bed of sawdust. When tested the day before it worked so instantaneously that even those prepared for the fact were startled by the suddenness of the fall.

Radcliffe turned around and said, "There, that is all they will see tomorrow."

December 1 dawned with a tremendous rain storm and presented a most dismal appearance. Buck was left alone with Father Cormier at 11 o'clock the night before and was awakened about seven o'clock in the morning. He said he had two or three naps during the night but that a pain in the back troubled him somewhat.

At half-past seven he took communion with Father Cormier. His breakfast consisted of three eggs upon toast and coffee, "a not extravagant bill of fare for his choice."

Buck ate heartily and dressed himself in a pair of dark striped pants and a white shirt, no other outside clothing. His boots were nicely polished. A short time later the ladies of the WCTU bade him farewell, this was followed by a solemn mass for the dead, in the cell.

In a brief conversation with, probably, the reporter for *The Transcript*, Buck is quoted as saying he only had a short time to live and he would "be damned glad to get out of this damned place."

There were, however, to be a few delays. First a variety of legal actions were required to be taken since the law had been changed and no death warrant had been issued. As a result, the sheriff was required to serve a number of documents to the witnesses, officials and to Buck himself until finally the death sentence was read.

Then, due to the rain, the sheriff postponed the execution for a half-hour.

The Gallows of New Brunswick

It was reported that there were tears in everyone's eyes as Buck
shook hands with everyone, including the executioner.
When the executioner, Radcliffe, had adjusted the noose and
stood waiting for the signal Buck said, "Let her go."
The sheriff gave the signal, the weight dropped and Buck
swung in the air and fell back in the flash of an eye.
A black flag hung limp and lifeless above the courthouse,
The Moncton Daily Transcript editorial headline noted:
A black flag is the only public sign of the tragedy
enacted in the name of the law.

Finally, at twenty-five minutes to ten the officials entered the corridor and Buck was brought from his cell. It was reported that there were tears in everyone's eyes as Buck shook hands with everyone, including the executioner, and the procession made its way to the gallows, led by Sheriff McQueen and Deputy Sheriff Wilson followed by Sheriff Freeze and Deputy Sheriff Keith; Jailer Tait and Dr. Teed, Father Cormier and Father Labbe, then the prisoner followed by Constables Wilber and Lawrence and the executioner, Radcliffe.

On reaching the scaffold Buck shook hands with the hangman again. With his legs pinioned and both priests beside him he listened as Father Cormier addressed the gathering and said:

"In the name of Buck my penitent, he asks forgiveness of all whom he has injured, and he also asks forgiveness of the world as he hopes God has forgiven him."

Buck kissed the crucifix and received the last consolation of the church.

When the black cap was being put over his head it did not seem at first to go on easy and Buck smiled. When the cap was placed and the noose was around his neck he said "Goodbye everybody. May God have mercy on me."

Dr. Gaudet said, "Go to heaven." And Buck replied, "Thank you."

When the executioner, Radcliffe, had adjusted the noose and stood waiting for the signal Buck said, "Let her go."

The sheriff gave the signal, "the weight dropped and Buck swung in the air and fell back in the flash of an eye. There was a convulsion, a tremor of the muscles for a second or two and then Buck was dead."

A black flag hung limp and lifeless above the courthouse, *The Moncton Daily Transcript* editorial headline noted: *A black flag is the only public sign of the tragedy enacted in the name of the law.*

This was not a popular hanging

From time to time there have been hangings in New Brunswick that were against the wishes of a large segment of the population. People who were convinced, despite due course of trial and juries, that the person to be hanged was not guilty of the crime for which they were being punished.

Such was the case of Thomas Francis Collins, accused of murdering Mary Ann McAulay, cousin and housekeeper of Rev. E. J. McAulay Roman Catholic priest in Irishtown, Albert County.

Collins' trials set and broke court records in Canada at the time and saw premiers of the province come and go before the case finally reached its unhappy, and controversial, ending on November 15, 1907.

A brief summary of the flight, capture and trials of Thomas Collins for the murder of Mary Ann McAulay follows. Collins' is a story that has been well chronicled over the years, particularly in Albert County publications. dd

On Thursday, August 23, 1906 the *St. John Globe* daily newspaper heralded the chase for Thomas Collins with the headline: "Chief and Detective Are on the Trail of a Suspect" then, in capital letters, "HE WAS AT MUSQUASH THIS MORNING."

Interest in the city was high since Mary Ann McAulay, who "was foully murdered," was a Saint John girl whose status was defined by the information that she was "related to Mr. Edward Hogan and Mrs. Joshua Ward."

The story briefly addressed Father McAulay's history as parish priest in New Ireland and went on to say "particulars of the terrible murder only add to the horror of the affair. It is now considered certain that the murder was committed in the woodshed of Father McAulay's home.

"On Monday afternoon at Elgin the priest met his former servant, Collins, who he had left at home. When questioned, Collins is alleged to have said, 'I had a row with the housekeeper'."

Since the previous Saturday Father McAulay had been touring his parish and beyond, organizing the annual church picnic. He left Elgin on Tuesday and arrived at his home around eight o'clock that night, driven there by James Doyle. The rectory was dark and silent on their arrival, the priest's horse was in the barn with part of its harness still on and the rectory door was unlocked.

Father McAulay went to his living area and discovered that an upper panel in the door of his bedroom closet had been cut up, presumably with an axe. There were other signs of disorder as well, which prompted he and Doyle to begin a search of the premises.

They went through the house carefully and discovered personal effects of both the priest and Mary Ann were missing, evidence of an earlier, hurried search. Mary Ann's money, her gold watch and a gold bracelet were missing but a cash box in Father McAulay's closet was not taken. They then went outside to the woodshed, examining it carefully before going to an opening in the floor that led to a small cellar. It was in this cellar that they found the body of Mary Ann.

She was fully dressed but had a gash in the back of her head, that appeared to have been made by an axe, the blade of which had crashed through her skull. In addition, her throat had been cut and the windpipe and artery were severed. There was a bruise on her right temple that looked as if it had been made by some blunt object, and both her hips bore marks of violence.

It appeared that the murderer left the rectory driving Father McAulay's team in the direction of Elgin via Little

River. It was supposed that at some point on the road, he turned the rig about and continued the journey on foot. The team was seen in the yard near the rectory by John Long on Monday morning . He said he thought that the priest was preparing to drive out. But the horse was seen again in the afternoon, this time without a carriage and only part of the harness. Thomas Mitton took charge of the animal and put it in the barn. He noticed the kitchen door of the rectory was open but saw no one. Not wanting to intrude he continued on his way. The carriage was found later at a watering place near the barn. It was presumed that the murderer, after leaving the horse, was given a lift along the road.

The *Globe* learned that Collins had supper on Monday evening at Darland's Hotel and subsequently made his way to Petitcodiac. On Tuesday he was seen at White's Mill then, in Petitcodiac, he bought a ticket for Saint John and left on the train at 10:10 Tuesday morning.

A jury was empanelled by Albert County coroner Dr. C.S. Murray and James Thean, foreman, John Duffy, Henry Doyle, James R. Long, Thomas Campbell, Arthur Huckins, and Michael Thean returned the following verdict:

"That said Miss Mary Ann McAulay was found dead on the 21st of August at New Ireland, Albert County and that the cause of death was that she had been murdered with an axe and that her throat was cut with a knife in the hands of some person unknown but we believe that that person is Thomas J. Collins, foreigner."

Although sightings of Collins were reported throughout the province, including in the jail at Sackville, the search was in earnest in the Saint John area. Fears were expressed that he had arrived on the Maritime Express on Tuesday afternoon in Saint John and had immediately left for the United Sates, walking towards Vanceboro, Maine.

Thomas Heenan, a railway lineman employed by Western Union Telegraph Company, was waiting near Dr. Walker's at South Bay when he was asked the way to Vanceboro by a man answering to the description of Collins. He described the man to be about 22 years old, short and with an impediment in his speech. He wore a short black coat, black trousers and new boots and was carrying his effects in an oilcloth bundle. His mouth was somewhat enlarged and generally fitted the description of Collins. Heenan said the man was anxious to "get across the line."

The next sighting in the chase was in Musquash and Police Chief Clark and Detective Killen from Saint John started off in pursuit. Another man, who arrived in the city the previous evening, reported to the police station that he had met a man he believed to be Collins in the vicinity of Spruce Lake on Tuesday. He confirmed the fellow was heading in the direction of Musquash. The police then communicated with a Mr. Dean and learned that the man, believed to be Collins, had been there that morning, Wednesday.

By Thursday the suspect had made his way through Lepreaux and men were on the lookout for him in St. George and area. Detective Killen was now on his own in the hunt with assistance from the local marshal and numerous volunteers along the way.

In the meantime the *Globe* had been attempting to discover something of Collins' background. They interviewed Capt. John Matthews, first officer of the *Edna M. Smith*, who said there was no one by the name of Collins who had come to Canada on board that vessel. However, there was a man who strongly resembled the man named Whitely, incarcerated in Sackville and still thought by some to be Collins.

Whitely came from Aberdeen under the name of "North" and was described as a "bad one ... with an unpleasant nature" by the captain.

As it turned out the real suspect, Thomas J. Collins, was the one working ... walking might be a better term ... his way through Charlotte County to the United States border.

During Friday afternoon a Mr. T.A. Sullivan, the proprietor of the Bonny River Hotel, was driving a party of tourists to Sparks Lake when he saw a man, who he instantly realized was Collins, making his way into a clump of bushes a short distance ahead of the team. A few minutes later he met Wilkes Reynolds and, leaving him in charge of the team, Sullivan went back for help. He found James Hill, Frank Kehoe and Alex Taylor and sent them to keep Collins in sight. Sullivan then sent to St. George for Detective Killen and Marshal McAdam who drove "as fast as horse could bear them" to the spot where Sullivan directed them, a couple of miles from what was called the "upper mill".

Sullivan then set out himself to catch up with the action. By the time the officers arrived Collins was already captured by the trio of Hill, Kehoe and Taylor. He was described as being "dusty, worn out both mentally and physically, and footsore. A very sorry spectacle." Sullivan told the *Globe.*

"His absolute loss of nerve made him a still more pitiable object. He wore a drab coloured shirt and coat, ordinary working clothes and hat. He carried his shoes in his hand and was scarcely able to walk so sore were his feet."

When searched Collins was found to have no money on him and, although he was wearing a silver watch, he did not have any of the stolen valuables in his possession. But he had left a valise at Councillor Dean's place in Musquash and it was believed they might be found in that. He did not deny who he was or that he had been employed by Father McAulay. He also admitted he had quarrelled with Miss McAulay but he was adamant in saying,

"I didn't commit no crime!"

He told the officers he had been born in Liverpool, England and came to Canada three months earlier, landing at Montreal on the steamer *Dominion*. His father was dead, he said. He did not know where his mother was. He made no pretence about wanting to reach St. Stephen and cross the border into the United States.

The *Globe* said that Chief Clark would join the other officers in St. Stephen but they would not return to Saint John with the prisoner until they had carried out a full investigation in that area.

"The importance of the case calls for a great amount of care being exercised in securing every jot of evidence possible. The officers, therefore, will ascertain as far as possible just what Collins' movements throughout the country were," the *Globe* opined.

By Sunday afternoon Collins had braved the scrutiny of the crowd waiting for him at the central police station in Saint John, and was duly photographed and questioned by the authorities. It was determined that his middle name was Francis, that he was single and, while he was a native of Liverpool, he was of Irish parentage and was a Roman Catholic. A small man, certainly by today's standards, Collins stood about five feet three and three-quarters inches, weighed 130 pounds, was of reddish complexion with black hair and grey eyes and with a full mouth. In addition to these physical attributes he had several tattoo marks and a scar of about one-eighth of an inch between the third and fourth fingers of his left hand.

According to the *Globe* ...

The Gallows of New Brunswick

...Collins, who persists in denying that he committed the murder, gave the officers the following account of his movements just before he left New Ireland and since that time..

During his stay with Father McAulay he said the housekeeper never let an opportunity pass when she might censure or accuse him. It had been her custom to refuse him food until he had performed his duties to her satisfaction. On Thursday she sent him to New Ireland Lake with instructions to catch a good mess of fish for use on Friday. He caught only four and this fact, he said, was sufficient to arouse the anger of Miss McAulay.

On Saturday after Father McAulay had left he arose and cleaned and fed the horses. One of the horses was at Mr. Duffy's, he alleges that he was subjected to another scolding from Miss McAulay. 'She called me a liar,' he said, 'and my reply was that I would see Father McAulay when he returned.'

After breakfast he chopped wood and stored it in the cellar.

Mr. Albert Gross then gave him a dollar on returning from fishing at the lake. Collins owed fifty cents to Mr. Duffy and as soon as Miss McAulay learned that he was in possession of money she told him somewhat abruptly to pay what he owed.

Saturday evening Mr. Thean and Mrs. Williamson, with members of their family, arrived for the purpose of fishing in New Ireland Lake the following day.

'On reaching the lake Miss McAulay told me to gather wood and start the fire going. I did as she said. After a while Mr. Thean and his son, Everett, and myself went out on the lake and fished. About 10:30 we all went to bed for the night.

'Next morning Mr. Thean and Everett and myself went fishing again. After breakfast Mr. Thean and Everett and myself went to the lake and stayed there until eleven. Some time after 2:30 o'clock the party drove back to the rectory. The Theans stayed for a while and, by and by, Mrs. Williamson left.'

Collins then went on to tell about Miss McAulay recommencing her advice about paying Mr. Duffy. Eventually Collins paid what he owed and says he was back at the rectory by 5:15 o'clock. After supper he visited for about an hour at the home of Mr. Williamson. The following morning he was up at six o'clock. At seven-thirty o'clock he was instructed by Miss McAulay to harness the horse for she wanted to drive to Elgin.

'I harnessed the horse but soon she came along and said she would not go –that the weather was too warm. Then came some rather warm discussion and finally I said I'd leave for I'd grown tired of having her shouting at me all the time. So I left the house and the last I saw of her she was alive and well.'

Collins told of how he walked to Elgin and to Petitcodiac where he took the train for Saint John. He said he knew nothing of Miss McAulay's death until he heard about it from the police. Detective Killen said when he was told why he was arrested Collins staggered and would have fallen had the detective not supported him. He tried to talk but was so overcome that his words were quite inaudible.

Nevertheless, during the drive from St. George Collins "sang a number of comic songs in good voice."

Despite mounting evidence to the contrary the *Globe* carried the following story on August 28.

VISITOR TO ALBERT TALKS OF THE MURDER

It would seem that popular opinion in the New Ireland murder case by no means fixes with certainty upon Collins, who is now under arrest as the perpetrator of the crime. Mr. Curtis Boisvert, of Portland, who returned on Monday from the section in which the crime was committed says that most of the area's residents do not believe he killed

Miss McAulay.

Mr. Boisvert, who travels in the interest of a cigar firm, spent last week in the immediate vicinity of the scene of the crime and talked to very many of the people. He says he only talked with one household who believe that Collins is guilty. He had become well known while at Father McAulay's and residents in the vicinity regard Collins as an injured man, in as much as they think he is not guilty of murder .... many of them do not hesitate in speaking of their suspicions of other parties than Collins.

Not all of the residents of the vicinity have been on good terms with the priest's household and certain of these are regarded as by no means beyond suspicion.

The Trials Begin

The preliminary hearing began in September and carried over until October 19, before Magistrate Stuart ruled that there was sufficient evidence for Collins to stand trial for Murder.

There were some big guns in the courtroom from the beginning, including the Premier of the province, Hon. L.J. Tweedie, and Clerk of the Peace Dixon who appeared for the Crown. The Premier had taken on the role of Crown Prosecutor and J.C. Sherren acted as defence counsel. Collins, according to the *Globe*, "took a great interest in all the proceedings and, for the most part, showed wonderful coolness."

The fact that it was the first murder to be tried in Albert County created great local interest, but the case held a public fascination far beyond that geographic border. It was not without its entrepreneurs who were quick to take advantage of the publicity. One man, a professional photographer, got special permission to have Collins brought from his cell early so he could pose him in front of the jail and take pictures of him. The photographs proved to be a hot souvenir item.

For the next few months Collins was destined to wait around in jail until the Albert sessions of the Circuit Court sat at Hopewell on January 15, 1907. Interest in the case remained high and more and more people became polarized in their verdicts of "guilty" or "not guilty."

The not guilty faction worked frantically at fund raising, intent on hiring the best defence they could find for

Collins. They succeeded in hiring Harrison A. McKeown, considered a brilliant lawyer of the time and J.C. Sherren remained as backup.

A St. Stephen native, McKeown had practised law at Saint John and during the 1890s represented the city and county in the Provincial Legislature and served in the cabinet as Solicitor General. Collins' supporters maintained that the province could send all the premiers it wished to Hopewell but it would have to go some to beat McKeown and Sherren.

The political pot was too hot in 1907 for the premier to follow up at the trial so the Crown called on Solicitor General W.P. Jones of Woodstock and C.N. Skinner, KC of Saint John to prosecute the case. Lawyers flocked to Hopewell to watch the proceedings.

Jury selection was the first hurdle to overcome. Mr. Justice George F. Gregory ruled that anyone who had contributed to the fund raised to pay Collins' lawyers was ineligible. There was considerable consternation on this count since many of those who contributed to the fund did so because they could see political motives behind the interest of the government's top guns, not because they necessarily saw Collins as innocent.

Perhaps one of the major questions posed the investigators of the murders was the location of the murder weapon. A dozen people, including detectives, claimed to have searched every nook and cranny of the house and premises for days without finding the axe. It wasn't until three weeks after Mabel Williamson, the daughter of the priest's nearest neighbours, came to work at the rectory that it was found.

Mabel found it barely hidden behind the commode in the priest's bedroom.

Detective Killen was so embarrassed that he said he'd have given several years of his career as a detective just to have been the one to have found it.

Collins' lawyer, McKeown, suggested that Collins "could not and indeed would not" have placed so obvious an object where and when the Crown claimed he did. He reminded the court of earlier testimony concerning a July break-in at the rectory and pointed out that both then, and during the weekend of the murder, it was common knowledge that the priest was away. He stressed that during the burglary, and no doubt on the occasion of the murder, Mary Ann had been absent from the house for a short time.

McKeown also did some detective work of his own and discovered that during the summer a pedlar was beaten and possibly robbed not far from the rectory. He made the case that the pedlar's assailant was the burglar, returned perhaps for more of the priest's good whiskey and, when taken by surprise, he became Mary Ann's murderer.

Dr. G.A. B. Addy, a pathologist brought in from Saint John, said that while the substance on the axe was dried blood he couldn't determine whether or not it was human blood. He went on to say that he could not find any traces of blood on Collins' clothing.

McKeown told the court that if, as the Crown contended, the axe had been placed behind the commode while still dripping with blood, there would have been bloodstains on the cotton cloth placed on the top of the commode to protect the wall. Dr. Addy said he could find no blood stains on the cloth. This, McKeown maintained, showed that the axe was placed there long after Collins had left New Ireland.

The trial lasted nine days. Although intense Collins remained cool, keeping his own transcript in the shorthand he taught himself during his months in prison. He regularly received mail from England and throughout Canada in support of his innocence.

In his summation McKeown made an emotional appeal after summing up the weaknesses in the Crown's case.

This boy has committed a crime of theft, he said, for which he deserves punishment. But has he committed a crime which necessitates digging a nameless grave on yonder hill, where his body shall lie until the Resurrection?

The judge, Mr. Justice Gregory, charged the jury the next morning, at which time he virtually condemned Collins from the Bench. He told the jury that it was his opinion that Collins first committed the murder "… with intent of robbery." He went on to say that Collins was a thief and that it was not a very great step from thief to murderer.

Exactly two hours later the jury returned with its verdict.

Guilty.

McKeown jumped to his feet then, very quietly, asked for a reserve case on the ground of judicial error in the charge. He quoted Mr. Justice Gregory as saying, "The prisoner's counsel is not bound to show that his client did not do the murder, but he is compelled to show that some one else did it."

He also added that throughout the trial the judge treated the guilt of the defendant as a proven fact, and directed the jury in the direction that the same person who broke the doors in the rectory was also the person who murdered Mary Ann McAulay.

The judge denied making the statement counsel attributed him and went about the further business of sentencing Collins to be hanged on Thursday, April 25.

A month later, during which Father McAulay died, the New Brunswick Court of Appeals decided unanimously that Thomas Collins should have a new trial, accepting McKeown's allegations.

Collins took it all in his stride and continued to read the books and magazines brought to him and playing a dart game he had designed from paper and pins. He also received regular mail from the Albert County ladies who were largely responsible for raising the money for his defence. The janitor said that from time to time Collins would conduct a Salvation Army service, doing the preaching, praying and the singing for an imaginary audience.

There were grumbles about the new trial from some of Albert County's taxpayers who felt it would cost them more money but William Pugsley, who had replaced L.J. Tweedie as premier in March, announced in the House that in this instance the provincial government would help relieve the burden and at least cover the costs of expert witnesses.

There were also those who maintained that Collins was guilty and that the whole procedure was a waste of time and money.

In addition, the political scene was in an uproar as scandals flew from one to another and premiers played musical chairs with the office of the Lieutenant-Governor. In the midst of it all McKeown married Grace Burpee, daughter of Mr. and Mrs. C.P. Burpee of Saint John, and took off for a European honeymoon tour. He did, however, get back in time for the new trial

The witnesses, including Collins, were well practised by now as were the attorneys and, in eight days, they were ready to sequester the jury. Chief Justice Tuck was careful not to suggest that Collins killed Mary Ann in his charge to the jury, but spoke every bit as harshly as had Judge Gregory against Collins. He dismissed Collins' story with sarcasm, suggesting that Collins "couldn't be believed." In closing he told the jury not to be swayed by any false sympathy.

Three hours later the jury reported that not only was it unable to agree but that there was no possibility of agreement.

The Chief Justice ordered them back to their deliberations for the night but next morning they reported that the vote remained at seven to five in favour of acquittal of Collins.

Chief Justice Tuck dismissed them and adjourned the new trial until September 17. It marked the first time in Canada a person was tried three times for the same murder.

Finding a jury was becoming an increasing problem.

Albert County had already set a record for all of Canada in calling 71 prospective jurors before finding 12 who claimed to have no bias. By now many prospective jurors were prejudiced, they had prejudged the case on the basis of common knowledge and published evidence; other prospective jurors were simply biased one way or another. Then it was discovered that a great many Albert County residents were opposed to the death penalty and could never support a guilty verdict whose outcome could call for execution of the prisoner. The numbers mounted, 121 prospective jurors were ordered to appear, 106 of these showed up and the court examined 100 of them before finding 12 they felt would serve without prejudice or bias.

Mr. Justice Daniel L. Hanington conducted the third trial. There was nothing new offered in this trial and he moved through the evidence quickly. Collins was not called to the stand, McKeown's defence summation was said to be brilliant and the judge's charges were found to be both lengthy and impartial.

Three hours and 35 minutes later the jury returned with its verdict. They found Collins guilty of murder.

"Pale but with marvellous composure and motionless and erect of figure, the youthful prisoner stood in the dock … as the fateful words were uttered, never once giving the slightest trace of emotion."

It was Tuesday, September 24 and Mr. Justice Hanington sentenced Thomas Francis Collins to be hanged on November 15, 1907.

Of the three possibilities of saving Collins from the gallows the chance of another successful appeal was discounted, there simply was no money available to pay for it. Nevertheless, Collins's supporters went door knocking again collecting names for a petition this time. Mr. Sherren took the petition to Ottawa on November 4, looking for the Cabinet to commute the sentence to life imprisonment.

The third resort was to have Collins declared insane.

On November 1 Dr. Edward Randall examined him and found him "soft on some points." At Sheriff Lynds' request (and it was rumoured also at his expense) two other specialists, Dr. S.C. Murray and Dr. John Lewis, were brought in. One said Collins was a moral degenerate without a proper sense of the enormity of his crime while the other found him lacking in some respects.

Sherren had no success in Ottawa.

Collins now had no options left but he did have a steady stream of sincere and caring visitors, a number of them clergy of various denominations including Rev. Byron H. Thomas, the Protestant chaplain at Dorchester Penitentiary, who spent hours with him and stayed until the final day.

On November 13 a stranger passed through Moncton and was duly noticed as he made his way to Hopewell in Albert County.

Thomas Radcliff was a short, fleshy, dark-moustached man, a man who was demanding and particular in his work. As hangman he was not impressed with the gallows sent from Dorchester to Hopewell. It was a gallows consisting of a horizontal beam with heavy weights at the short end and the rope at the long end. Radcliff maintained that it would have the effect of throwing the man too far in the air "with the probability of striking the beam overhead. He ordered an old-fashioned "drop" to be built instead.

The new scaffold was 11 ft. high and eight ft. square with the trap door in the centre. Because Collins was a small man and probably only weighted about 136 lbs, Radcliff said, he would need a nine and one-half foot fall to ensure his neck was broken.

That same afternoon Sheriff Lynds made a last ditch effort to save his prisoner. Based on the findings of the doctors who had examined Collins to determine his sanity Lynds had a government appointed alienist (psychiatrist) visit him. He declared Collins to be sane.

The hanging would go ahead the next day. Collins had

asked that he be hanged in daylight, not in the dark of the traditional hour after midnight.

He had numerous visitors during his final hours, Mrs. Isaiah Steeves, a woman who had been a leader in the effort to free him, said she came to bid the "generous, kind and very sensitive boy" farewell.

November 15, 1907, dawned clear and bright and, at 7:15 a.m. another visitor came to Collins' cell and shook his hand.

"Good morning Mr. Collins," said Thomas Radcliff.

"Good morning," replied Collins, shaking the hangman's hand.

His final handshake was also with Thomas Radcliff before he mounted the scaffold. Collins thanked Radcliff for all he had done and kissed him a tearful farewell, then stood quietly while his hands were manacled behind his back.

Collins walked to the scaffold with a firm and determined tread, a witness reported, mounting the steps unassisted.

At 7:25 a.m. his legs were pinioned and the black hood was drawn over his head. The chaplain began the Lord's Prayer and, at the words "deliver us from evil," the trap doors fell away.

Almost immediately two doctors, B.A. Marven and J.T. Lewis were beside the swaying figure beneath the platform. The hands twitched once or twice but after seven minutes they pronounced life extinct and the body was cut down and placed in a coffin.

Collins' body was then carried to the home of the jailor where it rested in the best room.

That afternoon the jailor's sitting room became a temporary chapel. Nearly 100 people crowded in and around the small home as Chaplain Thomas conducted a short funeral service. Many then followed the procession to the west corner of the jail yard. There, where a clump of evergreens stood, a grave had been made ready and they joined at the committal as Thomas Francis Collins' earthly trials finally ended.

Before Thomas Radcliff left Hopewell he said he found the hanging of Collins to be one of the most distasteful and disturbing tasks he had ever had to perform in his years as Canada's official hangman. He had not wanted to officiate, he said, but did so only after "urgent and repeated requests."

It is presumed those requests came from Sheriff Lynds, who would have had to hang Collins if Radcliff did not come.

The Bannister Boys
... Among NB's worst

"... ... a mother, almost naked, fleeing from her burning home in which her husband was scorching to a cinder, attempting to recover her stolen baby while, at the same time, carrying her other poorly-clad child, stumbling in the icy snow, getting up and going forward, over and over until she falls exhausted and dies: .... the little boy struggling futilely to scramble to his mother's body ...... only to fall and freeze to death."

This was the verbal image created in June of 1936 when Peter J. Hughes, Crown Prosecutor, addressed the jury for the last time in an attempt to have Daniel Bannister found guilty of the murder of Mr. Lake, the death of his wife Bertha and one child, the kidnapping of a second child and the burning of the Lake farm by the "Bannister Boys," Daniel and his younger brother Arthur. The entire event is a story more fascinating than the most gripping soap opera.

It all came about because Daniel and Arthur's mother, a manipulator bar none, wanted a real live baby to use as blackmail against a prominent businessman. The Lake family massacre was the result but it took two coroner's inquests, one trial by magistrate, two preliminary hearings, two sessions of the Appeals Court and four trials by a judge and jury before justice finally prevailed in Westmorland County.

Mrs. Bannister had already been sentenced. As one reporter put it, "the woman who, for a few dollars turned her own sons into kidnappers, arsonists and triple murderers was paying for her part in the crimes .... three and one-half years in prison, with time off for good behaviour."

Arthur had also finally been tried and sentenced to hang but the date was set ahead two months to August 20, because big brother Daniel had won a new trial. It was determined that the Chief Justice had "erred" when he "took from the jury the very point they had to decide, namely, whether the accused knew or ought to have known that murder was a possible consequence of any design which may have existed among the three with reference to the Lake baby."

So Arthur cooled his heels in Dorchester Penitentiary, just in case his testimony might be needed in Daniel's trial.

On June 26 the entire drama was presented again, this time before Mr. Justice Fairweather and a newly sworn jury. It was the seventh time most of the witnesses had told their story and it took until July 4 before Peter J. Hughes ran out of witnesses.

Daniel's brilliant defence lawyer, H.M. Lambert had no one to cross-examine, nothing to object about. It had all been done before, so he called his only witness, Daniel Bannister.

Daniel started off maintaining he did not know the purpose of the visits he, his sister and brother made to the Lake's home. He claimed that Mrs. Lake was supposed to be going to run away and he was only going up there with his sister Frances "for company." He also claimed to know nothing of a baby being brought home yet he, with his brother and sister, had carried the infant for eight miles.

He even denied ever giving the police a written statement, but admitted it was his signature on it. Why, he didn't even know a crime had been committed although he had already admitted to the Crown attorney that he knew there was evidence to directly link him to the crime.

The dramatic defence attorney had done his job well in the earlier trials but Peter Hughes was equally talented and he gave a vivid word picture of the events and, piece by piece, he shredded the testimony of the only defence witness. A very sober look replaced the vacuous grin Daniel had worn in the prisoner's dock.

Mr. Justice Fairweather told the jury that even if it felt Daniel Bannister bore less guilt than his brother, it could not return a verdict of manslaughter. It was "Murder or Nothing."

The public expected and wanted a quick verdict and they gathered in

Arthur Ellis, Canada's most famous hangman.

Dorchester's village square early in the evening. The jury came back at 9:45 p.m.

After 11 days of his second trial and six months to the day after the frozen Lake family corpses were found on the Ballast Pit Road, Daniel Bannister heard the foreman, Frank Tingley of Upper Dorchester, pronounce a single word: "Guilty."

The jury was polled and twelve times more he heard the word "Guilty." It was then his deadpan expression was replaced by a surly frown. When asked if he had anything to say before sentencing he replied "No Sir."

He stared straight ahead as sentence was pronounced and Daniel Bannister walked across the jail yard to his cell and to wait, with his brother, for the hangman on September 23.

Once again his lawyer appealed, this time to have the sentences of the two boys commuted to life imprisonment but on September 21 word came back from Ottawa. The appeal was refused and Daniel and Arthur awaited a more famous Arthur.

Arthur Ellis was Canada's most famous executioner. He had hanged or assisted at the executions of more than 600 people around the world by the time he had ended his career.

The sound of the carpenters building their gallows failed to spoil the appetites of the Bannister Boys, nor did it interfere with their sleep. Their two sisters, Frances and Marie and their father, William, visited them on the last day and reported that Daniel was cool and contemptuous but that Arthur was angry and bitter.

In the evening of September 22 the crowds began to gather once more. The RCMP moved in, some in scarlet dress uniforms, some in plain cloths. They would help keep the crowds back and assist inside the jail.

At 11 p.m. Constables Kent and Fenwick brought the brothers into the same room for the first time since early summer and the two-hour death watch began. Midnight passed and the crowd outside kept their quiet vigil. As 1 a.m. approached the procession formed inside the jail, Constable Kent and Arthur led the way followed by Constable Fenwick and Daniel followed by "Mr. Ellis." Sheriff I.N. Killam and the 14 official witnesses brought up the rear.

Both victims walked to the gallows in silence, their faces showing only their sullen resentment. They stood calmly and Mr. Ellis draped each head in a black hood and put the nooses in place.

Then Daniel made a request and it was granted.

His noose was loosened while he said a short prayer, and then tightened again.

Listeners could follow the proceedings easily. The doors used for the trap were used previously for a hanging in Amherst and, although they were well oiled and properly installed, the doors were heavy and the thunk of their falling echoed throughout the jail at 1:06 a.m.

The bodies of the two men were allowed to hang for 21 minutes when the hangman called "Lower Away" and the attendants took the remains of Daniel and Arthur Bannister from the gallows and placed them in coffins which had been left ready for the purpose.

An eyewitness was reported as saying that it was a weird scene, watching the two young men being carried to their last resting place in Potter's Field , a lonely spot on the hillside near the jail. It was here that a grave, measuring seven feet four inches long, six feet in width and four and one-half feet deep had been prepared for them. No relatives ever came to claim their bodies.

A battered, unclothed body ...... a quiet RAF sergeant hanged in St. Andrews

Bernice Connors and her friends were at the Community Hall in Blacks Harbour the evening of June 5, 1942. It was war time and, like girls around the world in those days, they were entertaining the young men in the armed forces stationed in their area.

That Friday night they were dancing and laughing and pretending for awhile that the war didn't exist. What did exist for them was that time and that place and the particular person they were dancing with at that moment.

No one remembered seeing Bernice after around nine o'clock. Her friends were having their own good time and, later, they just thought that one of the airmen she had been dancing with must have walked her home.

On Sunday, June 7, a Black's Harbour resident found a stray shoe on the road near Deadman's Harbour and took it home with him. His daughter recognized it as possibly belonging to a friend of hers, Bernice Connors. She promptly attempted to telephone her ... perhaps to tease her, perhaps simply to ask if she had lost a shoe recently.

Bernice's family, believing their daughter to be with friends or relatives, were alarmed when the shoe was found and made some calls of their own, to check their daughter's whereabouts. They were even more alarmed when they discovered she was at none of her usual weekend haunts. No one had seen Bernice, the attractive 19 year-old daughter of Mr. and Mrs. J. Edwin Connors, since Friday night.

Mr. and Mrs. Connors called Police Chief Dennis P. Guptill and reported her missing.

Chief Guptill began his search by walking up the road from where the shoe was found. He soon located the second shoe on the other side of the road, a short distance away. The ground there showed signs of activity that indicated a scuffling, possibly between two people. A short distance away there was a slight mound in the field that skirted the road.

The mound was covered with moss but, as he walked toward it, he could see a bare foot at the base. Four girls, friends of Bernice's who had followed along to help in the hunt almost stepped on the foot, they screamed and ran from the scene. Guptill brushed aside some of the covering dirt and discovered the body of Bernice Connors, naked save for a light garment thrown across her hips. She was lying on her back, her hands were folded across her chest and her eyes were staring upward, blind in death.

Further examination revealed that the back of her head was badly battered, as though by a rock or some similar rough implement, and there was evidence of severe head injury indicated by her badly swollen face and bleeding from the eyes nose and ears. Her throat was also cut.

Dr. H.S. Everett, coroner, called in a second coroner, John D. Mehan, Sr. who, with Harry M. Groom, Clerk of the Peace, held a brief inquest at Black's Harbour on Monday morning. Following this they then called in Dr. Arnold Branch, provincial pathologist, from Saint John and the body was removed to St. George where an autopsy was performed. Members of the coroner's jury included: Donald McLean, foreman, C.H. Brewer, James Cameron, Bert Gallagher, Ora Thompson, Lloyd Ingersoll and William Chisholm. The inquest was adjourned to June 16.

Also on Monday a police dog from Moncton was brought in to assist in tracking down the murderer. Anyone who appeared likely to be able to help with the case was questioned.

The RCMP investigating team, under the command of Sgt. Davis of the investigation department in Fredericton, determined that Bernice had left the Community Hall sometime between 10 p.m. Friday night and 1 a.m. Saturday when the dance broke up, and was not seen again until her body was found by Chief Guptill.

Dr. Arnold Branch told the inquest that during his examination of Bernice Connors' body he was struck by the appearance of her face and neck. The head was a bluish syanolic colour with oedematons. This swelling included lower eyelids and lips. There were indications of blood smears on ears. These smears did not include the streaks on the face.

Underneath her lower jaw there was a cut, two inches long. It had clean edges and clotted blood in the depth of the wound. A second cut was found on the inside of a gum and there was a cut in the front of the junction of lip and gum margin. The tongue was swollen and purplish in front.

Another small cut was on the left side of the scalp and in the region of this cut he found some material different from seaweed which, he thought, resembled rotten wood.

The only injury of any kind on the trunk was a contusion on one thigh.

Dr. Branch said the blood vessels of the brain were congested but with no marked haemorrhage. There was blood in the stomach and there was an "aroma suspicious of alcohol."

Specimens taken from the stomach and the heart showed traces of alcohol.

"I noticed when the abdomen was opened that it felt cold to the touch," he said but when asked by the clerk if the amount of alcohol in the victims blood could have caused her death he said, "No."

The cause of death, he said, was shock following head and neck injuries, alcohol in the stomach and blood and rape. When asked if there were lacerations in the vagina

Dr. Branch said, "Yes."

He went on to say the victim's wounds were caused by the use of brute force. None of her injuries could have been self-inflicted.

On June 19 the coroner's jury determined that Bernice Connors came to her death on the Deadman's Harbour Road, Black's Harbour between the hour of 9 p.m. June 5 and 9:30 p.m. June 7, 1942.

"We also agree her death was caused by injuries received as the result of a brutal attack inflicted upon her by a person or persons undisclosed."

On July 4 Sergeant Tom Roland Hutchings, a 21 year-old armourer in the Royal Air Force, stationed at Pennfield was committed to stand trial at the next court having criminal jurisdiction in the County of Charlotte for the murder of Bernice Connors.

Magistrate E.A. Nason called 36 witnesses against Hutchings before he was committed to jail to await trial. Hutchings had nothing to say and wanted no witnesses called in his behalf. He had counsel to represent him during the preliminary hearing.

The evidence presented against Hutchings included human blood stains on his Royal Air Force uniform; RCMP Detective Staff Sergeant F.W. Davis also collected various other articles of clothing including socks, underwear and shoes which he later turned over to RCMP Corporal Prime. In addition a stained "bluish" handkerchief, found near the kitchen door of the community hall in the morning of June 10 was discovered by Sgt. Davis and turned over to Dr. J.M. Roussel in Montreal. Also received in evidence were a ring from Hutchings' finger and a rock stained with blood found on the highway near the spot where the body was discovered.

Dr. Roussel advised the hearing that he had studied medico-legal work in Paris and, since 1932 had been associated with Dr. R. Fontaine in Montreal as an assistant.

He identified the uniform handed to him and said that although he could identify the blood stains on it as human he could not identify them by (blood) group.

Benjamin R. Guss of Saint John acted as counsel for Hutchings during his trial in October at which time he entered a not guilty plea. In defence of Hutchings Guss is quoted by the *St. Croix Courier* as having delivered "a spirited attack on the circumstantial evidence compiled by the Crown."

Guss questioned the time element of the case and repeated on several occasions that the Crown had failed to produce anyone who would testify that they had seen Hutchings kill or have improper relations with Bernice Connors.

"The Crown must produce evidence beyond a reasonable doubt that he is guilty," Guss said and quoted the medical evidence from Dr. Branch which showed that the girl might have been alive as late as Sunday afternoon.

"Someone may have seen her alive Sunday afternoon and had good reason not to come forward ... Reasonable doubt, the doctor's evidence was full of it."

He questioned whether a man unfamiliar with the area would choose the location where the body was found.

"There is more to this than meets the eye," Guss said. "A knife planted, seaweed, wet hair. It is not strong suspicion that justifies a jury in finding a man guilty. No man saw him do it. The issue of life or death is in your hands. Would you send him to a shameful death when the truth and nothing but the truth is known to God alone? You dare not do it," Guss told the jury.

Mr. Justice Richard took three and one-half hours in the late afternoon of October 6 to review the case in detail for the jury. He told them there were three conditions possible under which a verdict of "not guilty of murder" could not be returned.

The first of these was to find that the grievous injuries had not been inflicted on the body of Bernice Connors. The second was that the jury should find that such injuries had been inflicted, but not by the accused. The third, the finding that such injuries had been inflicted by the accused but did not cause the girl's death.

"Assuming that the above mentioned three findings have been made in effect, the verdict of 'guilty of murder' comes in for consideration."

He addressed the possibilities of a manslaughter verdict and warned the jurors of prejudicial judgement based on hostility against the accused. "You must not be influenced by prejudice on one hand or sympathy on the other. Your decision must be determined by what you have heard in this court. ......

"The accused is innocent until proven guilty and the burden is on the Crown to prove guilt. The Crown must prove the case beyond a reasonable doubt ... the doubt must be real, not something fanciful so as to prevent you doing your duty."

After three hours of deliberation the jury returned a verdict of guilty against Tom Hutchings, but they asked for mercy.

On October 6, 1942, Mr. Justice Richards said he was bound by law to pass one sentence and one sentence only. "The sentence of this court is that you be taken to the common jail for the county of Charlotte the place from which you came and on Wednesday the 16th day of December next be taken to a place of execution and there hanged by the neck until you are dead."

Although the jury recommended mercy the Secretary of State's department of remissions, on reviewing the case, sent out official notice that Tom Roland Hutchings should be hanged for his crime.

At 1:46 a.m. on Wednesday, December 16, 1942 Tom Roland Hutchings of Peterboro, England went to his death calmly at St. Andrews. C.L. Woods, witness to the hanging and writing in the *Telegraph Journal* on December 17, 1942 said Hutchings "with firm step ... walked from his cell in the Charlotte County jail here at 1:46 a.m. today. Two minutes later he walked up the 18 steps leading to the scaffold within the confines of the jail yard, and two minutes later the trap was sprung, the former R.A. F. Sergeant paying with his life for the murder of 19 year-old Bernice Connors, Black's Harbour, last June.

"Life was pronounced extinct at 2:02 a.m. by Dr. H. P. O'Neill, St. Andrews, jail physician and Dr. R. A. Massie, St. George.

"The stockily built young man who showed no emotion throughout his preliminary hearing and trial, maintained his nonchalant attitude to the end, and as he left his cell for the last time he pulled the electric light cord, turning out the light, and walked between his guards through the narrow corridor of the jail into the yard. He looked straight ahead to the scaffold and never hesitated, walking steadily up the steps and on to the trap which minutes later dropped him to eternity in early punishment for the death of the young woman he had met at a dance in the Black's Harbour community hall a few months ago."

Hutchings went to his death wearing the slacks and tunic of his Royal Air Force uniform. He made no statement prior to leaving his cell or while on the scaffold. He stood very still after being escorted to the gallows, tilted his chin high as the black hood was placed over him, and seconds later dropped to his death.

His last visitors were Squadron Leader Mann and Squadron Leader Stewart, chaplain and medical officer from the RAF station at Pennfield. Squadron Leader Stewart accompanied Hutchings to the gallows.

Hutchings made no statement prior to his death. He remained cheerful to the last, and last evening whistled merrily in his cell a few short hours before the law exacted its penalty for the brutal crime.

That morning official notice was posted on the door of the jail notifying the general public that the execution had been carried out according to law and at 10 o'clock a coroner's jury conducted an official inquiry as prescribed by the law, before Dr. F.V. Maxwell, St. George.

For several hours prior to the execution RCMP patrolled the area in the immediate vicinity of the court house and jail and no person was allowed to loiter. Sheriff Charles W. Mallory did not reveal the hour of the execution and only official witnesses, two doctors and C.L. Wood, *Telegraph Journal* reporter, were present in the court yard when the trap was sprung. Camille Blanchard of Montreal was the hangman.

Hutchings' execution was the first in Charlotte County since Thomas Dowd was hanged 65 years earlier.

New Brunswick's last gallows

On February 10, 1957 a 14 year-old boy, Kenneth Laakso, saw a depression in the snow of Petrie Lane, Charlo Station. The depression, he later told the court at the murder trial of Joseph-Pierre Richard, was the same shape as a giant egg. Curious, he stepped in it only to discover he was standing in something both hard and soft. Stepping off the object he bent to brush the snow away and discovered the body of 12-year-old Katherine de la Perelle.

She was a mere 100 yards from her home.

The night before, Saturday, February 9, Kate and some friends were working on Valentines and a Valentine Box for school the next week. At 10:30 p.m. she left the Vincent family home and began the short walk to her own home, stopping to buy a five cent bag of peanuts at a convenience store 400 yards from the de la Perelle home.

Depending on the reports one reads Richard was 1: lurking outside the Vincent house that night and was seen by both the victim and her friends (according to evidence contained in a story written by Alan Hustak in 1987) or 2: was the "stranger" seen "by friends" both in the area of and inside the convenience store where she purchased her peanuts (as reported in the Moncton Daily Times on Monday morning February 11,1957). Yet no evidence identifying these persons as Richard was offered in the course of the two trials needed to convict him of Kate's murder and eventually see him hanged on December 11, 1957.

When Kate failed to return home by 11 p.m. Saturday night her family began to check on her whereabouts. They learned that she left the Vincent home at 10:30 p.m.

They eventually contacted the RCMP and instigated a search for their daughter. A foot of snow fell during the night and hampered their search, completely covering the body, and obliterating both footprints and scents that might have helped the search dog in its quest and the RCMP in their investigation.

There was little question but that the community had made up its collective mind that Richard was the killer. The problem they, and the RCMP, faced was a total lack of tangible evidence; evidence placing him at the scene of the crime; evidence of a motive for the killing. Evidence of any kind, other than circumstantial.

The community was frustrated by what was apparent to them and would eventually prove damning to Joseph-Pierre Richard ... his official police record and local reputation.

Described as thickset, bull-shouldered and beetle-browed with shifty eyes Richard had been recently been released from prison, where he had been serving a three-year sentence for the attempted murder of a taxi driver, Théophile Gallant.

Four years earlier Richard had asked Gallant to drive him to pick up a package. It was said later that he suspected Gallant (a married man with a child) was having an affair with his, Richard's, wife. Gallant stopped to relieve himself on a lonely side road off Highway 11 and Richard shot him with a 20-gauge shotgun. The injured Gallant escaped into the surrounding woods and made his way to an Anglican rectory where a priest contacted the RCMP.

Richard was arrested, charged with attempted murder and pleaded guilty. Judge Enoel Michaud was lenient with him, offering him a chance to mend his ways by sentencing him to three years behind bars. A sentence and decision not popular in this northeastern community which was already apprehensive when Richard was paroled and returned to the area in December of 1956, a few short weeks before Kate de la Perelle was found murdered.

The people of Charlo believed Richard had "got away with murder" once. They told their children he was the devil and that he stalked the countryside at night. They told the RCMP and the media their concerns, that they could not understand the lack of action in arresting him.

Kate de la Perelle passed Richard's house every day on her way to school, she knew his children and talked to them often and she knew Richard and did not fear him.

While the community voiced its concern the RCMP attempted to build a case strong enough to arrest Richard and charge him with murder. One officer, Constable Harold Warren Burkholder firmly believed that no murderer could leave a crime without leaving some evidence behind him. To this end he began a meticulous search shovelling, raking and sifting through the snow in Petrie Lane. He was rewarded with a button and three human hairs.

Armed with these clues, and a description of the coat Richard was said to be wearing when he was seen outside the Vincent house the night Kate was killed, RCMP Sergeant David Bryenton went to Richard's home and asked to see his coat. Richard claimed his coat had been burned by coal acid and that he had buried it in the snow near the railroad track.

They did not arrest Richard at the time but asked him to come voluntarily to the police station. Richard complied, and he was held there for two days where he slept on a chesterfield in a small room. which he was not permitted to leave. The RCMP found the coat, with four buttons missing and an intact fur collar embedded with a red fuzz which resembled the material of a sweater Kate was wearing when she was killed. The coat was actually found in the ice of the Charlo River, downstream from where Richard had said he buried it.

"Tell us the rest of the story," they said to Richard after finding the coat.

Richard said if they proved their case and he was sentenced he would tell them before he died. He then began to cry. He was charged with the murder of Katherine de la Perelle and formally arrested.

He was defended by Campbellton lawyer Wilfrid Senechal who is quoted as saying that his client had an undeveloped conscience and his only redeeming feature was that he "was not very bright."

Despite this, Senechal did his job well. Throughout the trial he wove a pattern that suggested that Richard had been pre-tried and prejudged by the community because the town was afraid of him. In his address to the jury he stressed that there was no evidence to directly link Richard to the murder. Neither the coat the police had found nor the meticulous detective work that "unsnowed" pubic hairs that would appear to match Richard's were sufficiently identified as his. (In today's world DNA would quickly determine his guilt or innocence on these items alone.) All the evidence was circumstantial, he told the jury.

Judge Michaud advised the jury that if the circumstantial evidence was strong enough to satisfy them, with moral certainty, as to what had actually happened it would be sufficient to find a guilty plea.

The jury found him guilty and Judge Michaud, the same judge so generous in sentencing Richard in the earlier crime, to which he had confessed, now sentence him to be hanged on July 17.

Senechal appealed and the appeal was granted, on the basis that the primary duty of a law enforcement officer is not to obtain conviction but to ensure that justice is done. A duty not performed by the RCMP when they detained Richard for two days without arresting him. The New Brunswick Court of Appeal further agreed with Senechal that the fact that Richard was crying and looking at snapshots from his wallet when he made the statement that if he was sentenced then he would tell them what happened before he died, indicated that he had been subjected to a process akin to brainwashing.

Richard's family was threatened, his lawyer was threatened and told that if he got Richard off the second time he, Senechal, would be the one hanged.

Jury selection was difficult, more than 80 persons were questioned before 12 were found suitable to act. They, too, found Richard guilty.

Before sentencing him Mr. Justice C.J. Jones asked Richard if he had anything to say. Richard replied:
All I can say is that I ain't guilty. I didn't kill that little girl."

He was then sentenced to be hanged on December 11, 1957.

An anonymous hangman, said to be from Montreal, arrived in Dalhousie on Monday, Dec. 9, 1957. He, along with the witnesses; Sheriff Edmund LeBlanc, two RCMP officers, jailer Daniel Dewar, Father Benoit and Dr. Bujold; Dr. Potter's jury including Donald Mealy, Edrick Allain, Walter Mott, Walter Savoy, Wendell Firlotte and Louis Allard, all of Dalhousie, and Dr. Arthur Roy along with a spare juryman, if needed, Amede Doucette of Campbellton completed the required minimum panel and arrived at the Restigouche County jail before 11:30 p.m. on the evening of December 10.

An additional witness was Katherine de la Perelle's father, who had asked to be present.

Father Benoit said the mass in Joseph Pierre Richard's cell and Richard received communion and one of the two injections of morphine he had been allotted for this night.

According to a statement attributed to Sheriff LeBlanc in *They were Hanged* the gallows was built right in the sheriff's office. A hole was cut through the floor and a gallows erected above it. Sheriff LeBlanc opened the door from his office and called out: Joe, come on out.

Richard came out, took one step down from the jail into the sheriff's office and then took three steps up to the gallows. He had a picture of his newborn baby in his shirt pocket, next to his heart.

He appeared calm, according to the sheriff's account and at the allotted time of 12.05 a.m he said he hoped the Lord would forgive as the trap door opened and his body dropped down to eternity in the basement of jail. He was later buried in the cemetery at Nash Creek.

No, Joseph-Pierre Richard, did not confess to killing Katherine de la Perlette, unless it was to his confessor in the sanctity of the confessional.

But his was the last hanging to be carried out in the province of New Brunswick.

About the Author

Dorothy Dearborn began writing as a child and published her first poetry and short stories in the 1950s. A television career in the 1960s was interrupted by six years of front-line political involvement.

She worked for eight years as a reporter and in various editorial positions, including that of city editor, at *The Evening Times Globe* and was editor of the weekly newspapers *The Kings County Record* and *The Saint John Citizen*.

Among her many interests are the promotion of adult literacy and human rights in New Brunswick and an often frustrating romance with Duplicate Bridge.

Mrs. Dearborn's work may be found in numerous regional, national and international newspapers and magazines, including *We're Home*, a New Brunswick magazine she publishes and edits.

When not travelling the province researching and collecting stories and information for her work she can be found in front of her Macintosh computer at the family's 19th century farmhouse in Hampton, in the company of her ancient pony 'Soupy' and surrounded by a motley assortment of other critters.

She is married to Fred Dearborn, they have four grown children and numerous grandchildren.

About the Illustrator

Carol Taylor, who has illustrated six of Mrs. Dearborn's books, is well known throughout the Maritime Provinces for her outstanding, three dimensional art primarily using clay as her medium. An outstanding example of her work may be seen highlighting the clock over the Germain Street entrance of the Saint John City Market.